1

The Art of Impactful Communication:

How to Genuinely and Effectively Connect, Talk to be Heard, and Create Remarkable Relationships

by Patrick King

www.patrickkingconsulting.com

Table of Contents

Introduction

One of my best friends is named Jason, and I met him because we were on the same soccer team. (That sounds like something a five-year-old would say.)

I take my hobbies pretty seriously, which meant that when I was younger, I was playing soccer at least five days a week and mostly with the same people. We would spend a couple of hours scrimmaging and playing other teams, and then afterward, we would almost always go out for dinner. It was during one of those dinners that I had the good fortune of being seated next to Jason. This is when our friendship began.

However, here's a secret I only told Jason after I'd known him for over a year: I absolutely hated him when I first met him. It wasn't a slight aversion, a small annoyance, or just a pebble in my shoe.

He made a spectacularly negative impression on me for reasons that I couldn't quite articulate. We had differing views on everything, but that alone wasn't an issue. Something about him just rubbed me the wrong way—probably a familiar feeling for everyone.

The first time we met, he was seated on my right, and I spent the majority of the dinner heavily tilted to my left side, trying to pretend he didn't exist. I don't remember much in particular about that night except thinking to myself while walking to my car, "That Jason guy was annoying. I need to claim my seat faster at dinner so I don't sit next to him again."

Luckily for future Patrick and future Jason, we were forced into constant interaction because of our respective dedication to soccer. Big groups, small groups, it didn't matter. I ended up seeing Jason at least twice a week for a series of months, and I did my best to ignore him based on the first impression he had made on me.

Everyone else seemed to enjoy interacting with him, so at some point, curiosity got the better of me and I didn't rush to avoid him at our next regular dinner.

It turned out that we had a mutual love for fantasy basketball, which had never before come up in conversation. This made the difference in how I viewed him, as we instantly jumped into a rousing conversation about the valuation of players and potential trades. We were able to bond over a mutual interest and I was able to completely forget about the negative impression I previously had about him.

We exchanged contact information so we could talk about strategies and statistics later that night, and a friendship was born.

What does this have to do with the subject of this book on communication and relationships? Isn't my friendship with Jason a direct oxymoron of good communication because it literally took us months to connect after initial phases of judgment? It is, and that's the point.

My and Jason's friendship is an outlier to the harsh reality of meeting new people: if you don't make a positive first impression, you simply won't be friends. If the initial communication falls flat, most of the time, the relationship won't get a second chance. We were forced into each other's proximity for months, which isn't a luxury other people have. This allowed us to be an exception where other people would simply never look back.

Multitudes of studies have shown that people live and die by snap judgments they make about others within seconds of meeting someone new. How quickly are these judgments made? Sixty seconds? Twenty? A 2006 study by researchers at Princeton University determined that first impressions were made in roughly one-tenth of a second. That's not a lot of wiggle room. People decide whether or not they want to invest more time in you immediately. It's unfair, but it's reality, and it determines the fate of a friendship immediately. That's the importance of the first impression and communication in general.

Communication not only makes you friends; it gives you second and third chances to salvage potential connections. And of course, communication takes those relationships from passing to close and intimate.

Jason and I got what very few people get in this world—a second chance. We were forced to interact so much and so frequently that we were able to overcome any negative first impressions that existed. I very nearly missed out on the best friend that I have and someone who I have no doubt will be a groomsman at my wedding.

In all respects, communication benefits your life. Think about the last supervisor you had, however. Were they necessarily better than you at your job? Could they do everything better and more quickly than you?

Probably not. However, they were almost

certainly in good graces with the people that matter and knew more people that had the power to make decisions. It turns out that likability, not technical ability, is a big part of the job description in management and getting promotions. People wanted to deal with them first and foremost, and the rest, like technical abilities, people can always learn on the job. They can't easily learn social grace, however.

That's why business is the epitome of "It's not what you know but who you know." Revenue flows through communication, no matter the ability.

Communication even helps your health. Studies have shown that the number one factor for happiness in the elderly is how many strong relationships they have. This makes perfect sense: at an advanced age, everything except the people in your life and your relationships are ephemeral and temporary.

Generally, we tend to instantly put people into one of three buckets:

1. People we like
2. People who made no impression whatsoever
3. People we don't like

That's in the best-case scenarios. The middle bucket might be something you can wiggle your way out of and into the first bucket. However, more and more, because people simply don't have the time and energy to filter people properly, things are increasingly shaping up to be a two-bucket world with the first and third buckets only.

As with most valuable life skills, you were likely never taught how to communicate effectively. You may have learned how to communicate a message, but a message without the proper delivery, tone, and style will always fall upon deaf ears.

If you take nothing else from this book, communication, for all intents and purposes, is the gatekeeper to the life you want. It is what opens doors, creates relationships, and allows you to navigate the world in the social way that humans were meant to.

Chapter 1. It's All About Your Approach

We've established that communication is going to be one of the gatekeepers to just about everything you want in life. This seems to be at odds from what we've heard since childhood: that the world is a meritocracy and that we need to work hard to give ourselves the best chances for success. What gives?

Well, those two proposals can both be true simultaneously. The harder you work, the more quickly you will rise. Life *can* be meritocratic when you just start. But at a certain point, your personal relationships will determine where you will ultimately end up professionally. And of course, this is not even mentioning that your social life and network of friends is entirely dependent on your ability to build relationships through nurturing and respectful communication.

Communication is much more than the words coming out of your mouth or sliding into your ears. It is the ability to create something from nothing and, in the same vein, reduce something to nothing.

Imagine that you're in a foreign country where you don't speak the language. It's frustrating and you have difficulty communicating anything. You're not sure if people are getting your message. Now imagine that you have a vocabulary of around 100 words. You can communicate most messages in a roundabout way, and you won't starve to death. You can generally accomplish what you need, though there will be a significant number of misunderstandings and inefficiencies.

Many of us are stuck at that 100-word vocabulary level—even when we are all speaking the same language. In other words, we simply don't have the tools to communicate fluently even though we think we do.

The first step to fixing that is to address your general mindset and perspective on better communication. As with all actions, communication begins with your choices, and all the techniques at gaining rapport and connecting with people will do you no good if you can't commit yourself to the mindset of better communication.

So what are the patterns of thought that can help you become a better communicator without even lifting a finger? The first one might be counterintuitive, but it's about being an intentional communicator instead of passively waiting for opportunities to connect with people.

Being Intentional

Think back to the circumstances you met one of your best friends in. How did it happen? Did you see a toddler from across the room and decide that he was going to be your best friend?

It was probably random chance. It was a strike of lightning, a stroke of luck, that you sat next to someone. They mentioned something that interested you, and you replied with something that made them interested. Jimmy sat next to you and made a comment about how he liked turtles and you also happened to like turtles, or Janet asked if she could braid your hair and you said yes because you were bored.

Maybe it was a happenstance and unpredictable situation that was lucky to come to fruition. You weren't aware of what you were doing, so it just happened by accident. You weren't trying to connect intentionally or by design. You were flying by the seat of your pants and hoping that you were going to be lucky and connect with others.

For most of us, this is how we think friendships happen—by strokes of luck that we have no control over. Thinking that friendships only occur naturally is like going into a job interview and only hoping and praying you get asked the right questions and that the interviewer doesn't ask you about your prior criminal convictions. You're not preparing yourself for success, and you're relying upon a fortunate sequence of events that are out of your control.

This is why a common complaint among over the over-30 crowd is how difficult it is to meet friends and create new relationships. It's because you don't realize how big of a role you must intentionally play in it.

You might look at this as a long-winded way of emphasizing the importance of being intentional about how relationships are formed and attempting to communicate intentionally rather than by luck or *fate*.

Not being intentional about connecting and communicating makes us waste the interactions we do have because we passively accept that it may not lead to anything and thus are led to inaction.

The point is this: if you see connection and communication as dependent on luck and circumstances, you are creating an invisible prison for yourself. If you think things like "I only get along with people who are X" or "People who are Y annoy me," you're prematurely shutting the door on people and giving yourself an excuse not to reach out and take an interest in others.

It's no different than trying out for a basketball team, not making the cut, then proclaiming that you weren't really interested in making the team and you were just doing it as a joke. You're putting yourself at the mercy of your surroundings and circumstances, which builds a mental dependency or crutch.

This creates a self-fulfilling prophecy where we find failure because we fixate on it. Naturally, this can prevent relationship-creating any time the right mixture isn't present. Truly organic situations for you to seamlessly step into a conversation or engage a stranger are inconvenient at best and impossible at worst. For example:

- You assume you can only talk to people if they are interested in soccer.

- You assume you can only start a conversation with a stranger if there is a compelling need or reason.
- You assume you don't get along with certain types of people.
- You assume people aren't interested in knowing you.
- You assume small talk can't lead anywhere deeper.
- You assume this particular circumstance isn't ideal for meeting people.

Notice that these are all assumptions that cause you to tie your own hands.

The potential reasons for not attempting to connect are endless, but they only serve to put you into a mindset of passivity. Think about how differently the above situations would turn out if you start embodying the mindset to communicate intentionally rather than by luck. You would act more often than not, and that can make all the difference.

When you walk into a roomful of strangers, you don't need an opening or cue to proceed. You don't need any of elements that make you feel more comfortable "organically" connecting. You don't even need to feel like you have much in common or that you will be lifelong friends. These things are all holding you back.

When was the last time a new person came into your group of friends? How were they accepted and why? Was there an initiation ritual, or did you all discuss afterward and vote the new friend in as a member of your social circle? How were they able to penetrate the circle?

On your end, it was just a matter of people being open-minded and accepting. On their end, it was likely a conscious effort to integrate. They shared information about themselves and showed interest in the people in your group. They connected on common themes and interests and talked about shared values and aspirations. They shared news and gossip while pretending to be nonjudgmental. They knew they needed to achieve a certain velocity.

They were a single dot on the outside of a

circle, so they had to be intentional about their communication and truly put in an effort. Perhaps that's the best way to view the relationships in our lives—both current and future. We're always trying to gain the sufficient velocity to break them in one way or another. Sometimes, sharing a similarity such as being a science fiction fanatic can give us such velocity. But most of the time, you'll have to generate it on your own by being intentional.

Change Your Goals

This next mindset for successful communication is about goals, which again sounds counterintuitive. Goals color the way in which we approach communication and relationships. At the outset, most of us have the goal to impress others, thinking that this will make us more eligible in friendship. We want to make a good impression, so naturally we want to present ourselves in the best light possible.

However natural this feels to do, it's not quite as effective as you might think outside of a job interview. The approach of impressing someone just doesn't translate too well to most contexts. We want to show that we're worthy of being a friend, and even attractive, because of what we have to offer. But very rarely do we make friends based on those criteria.

Instead, what do we make friends based on? In the previous section, you learned that it's about being available and making effort. That's the crux of being intentional with communication. You can't passively expect things to happen, because you'll be waiting a long, long time.

We don't make friends based on that many aspects. Sometimes we have more value-based, transactional relationships, but we probably don't consider them our close friends. Instead, our close friends are who they are because they either entertain us or engage us. These are the bulk of our daily interactions that draw us closer to one person versus another. We like being around them, the feeling is mutual, and you walk away with feelings of pleasure and happiness.

Nothing may be particularly memorable or exciting, but instead you feel comfortable, familiar, and happy.

Thus, we need to reevaluate our goal orientation in communicating. We need to look past impressing people and more toward being the person who creates the same feelings of comfort, familiarity, engagement, and happiness.

What actually happens when you try to impress someone—besides the risk that you may turn people off with your ego and bragging? You spend time talking about yourself, talking yourself up, and describing unique experiences you've had. You don't pay too much attention to the other person, and you generally make yourself the hero of the conversation.

You focus on the stories that make people gasp, and these stories are always unrelatable for other people. In fact, the more unrelatable, the bigger the impressed gasp of a reaction you will receive at your story, so you strive to sound as unique as possible. This is all great for a moment, and it might indeed impress the other person. But what after? Where does the conversation go after you've learned about someone's impressive and unique experiences? You haven't actually learned much about them, and you haven't shared about yourself yet.

When you seek to impress, there's no room for finding similarities or engagement. The very goal of impressing is to share an experience that is foreign and alien. You're just trying to capitalize on shock value. What about the common ground and the feelings we talked about before: comfort, familiarity, engagement, and happiness? Those certainly don't spring from being someone's audience and marveling at their achievements, which is what happens when you seek to impress people.

Who cares about someone's unique experiences if you don't have anything in common with them? That's the crux of why you should forget about impressing and reorient your goals. Focus on the things that bond people together in everyday life— commonalities, both positive and negative—and you'll find friends quicker than by being the dancing monkey telling stories.

In the same vein, if you're not trying to impress someone with your experiences and stories, you might be trying to impress with your wit and intelligence. That's equally detrimental to creating a bond with someone because it means you're still focusing on putting yourself into a certain light instead of reacting to the person in front of you. A theme that will run throughout this book is that most people's communication is far too self-focused. But as someone far brighter than I quoted, "Two monologues don't make a dialogue."

One specific way to realign your communication goals is to focus on *amusement* for both parties of a conversation. Specifically, amuse yourself and entertain others in the process. Communication should be to (1) make it fun for yourself and (2) make it fun for other people.

Put another way, your goal when you speak

to other people in a social setting should be to engage them and make it *not boring* for them and yourself. It might sound like a tall task, but this is an easier goal because there are literally infinite ways to accomplish this as opposed to impressing others.

When you focus on amusing *yourself*, suddenly many filters are removed because you just want to ask or comment on what interests you. Likewise, when you focus on entertaining others, you're less inclined to stay on surface-level small talk and engage in topics that are personal and varied.

Boring is death. You might have other goals in mind, but if you just provide an interaction that people are entertained by, it will be mutually enjoyable and anything else you want from it will flow naturally. Just like if you want to make more sales or connect in a business context, people are going to be more willing to do so if they enjoy interacting with you.

Many people drift from interaction to interaction without a goal or purpose and are content to be unmemorable. Indeed, cultivating an air of self-amusement and entertainment can sometimes happen organically, but there are a few mindsets you can borrow to simply have more fun and less boring conversations. It would be nice if we could just wait for a mutually interesting topic to arise, but that's an attitude that is passive and puts you at the mercy of Lady Luck or other people making the effort. Instead, be proactive and manufacture the type of interaction you want by making the first move.

If you're in a boring conversation, you're at least 50% responsible. You have the power to control a conversation and make it as entertaining or probing as you want, so seize the reins and don't rely on others to entertain you. Embody the mindset that you possess the power to change your circumstances.

Understand that everyone possesses a fun side and desires to be entertained.

They may not show it readily, or they may hide it under a professional façade, but what you see is not always what you get.

For example, many people say they feel constrained at the workplace because they feel the need to be overly appropriate with their coworkers, but their coworkers are people too, and they have friends who act in silly ways. And yet, people tend to act in a freer and more unfiltered manner with anyone besides their coworkers. Point being, you may need to dig a little bit and find their quirky and fun sides, because for any number of reasons, they are keeping it subtle or holding back.

To be entertaining (to others) and amusing (to yourself), it's your duty to dig below the surface and find what makes people beautifully abnormal or noteworthy. These are the personal differences that give us our identities and, more importantly, provide fodder for fun and playful conversation material.

Self-amusement begins with viewing others as opportunities to interact, like a video game where you want to discover how much of your surroundings will react to you. Develop the mindset of interacting with people and things in your daily life just to see what happens when you *poke* them, and it will serve you well in conversations.

Do you feel differently about coffee than Johnny? Why does he hate it and refuse to drink it under any circumstances?

Does someone comb their hair in a particular way? When did they start to do that? What's the story behind it, and why does it differ from your method?

Dig into people and their differences and share your own unconventional methods or views on a subject. This strays from the norm and will make people react in ways that break their scripts and templates. In other words: a conversation they haven't encountered before and one that isn't boring.

This brings up another common theme: the way people actually connect with others is through engagement, entertainment value, and comfort. You don't become friends with someone because they meet your ideals or standards.

Filter your thoughts less. See what reactions you can provoke. Ask ridiculous hypotheticals. Seek to find the humor in any situation. Ask what hilarious situations something you see reminds you of. Compare an innocent bystander to a Disney character. Answer questions with movie references. Think out loud.

The common theme is you are the one initiating it. You can't rely on others to do the work for you or expect to be entertained by others like a sultan. When you shoot for self-amusement and entertainment, connection and engagement occur as a by-product.

Stay Curious

The third mindset for better communication is about curiosity. You can be the most charming, funniest person in the room, but if you aren't *interested and curious* about the person across from you, there simply won't be a connection. Again, this goes back to focusing on others and putting yourself onto the back burner.

Staying curious is a difficult proposition because, at first glance, most people might seem uninteresting or unworthy of paying attention to. This is undoubtedly the biggest hurdle for most of us—even if you don't consciously think it, you subconsciously believe that someone is not worth being curious about. You think that even if you dig deeper, you won't find anything worth your time, so why bother in the first place?

It's true that, at first glance, very few of us are compelling. But acting on this impulse will limit your communication and keep you right where you are. Changing this belief is a topic for another book, and in the end, it doesn't particularly matter what you believe. Just start digging deeper to build the habit of curiosity, and eventually it won't matter if you think people are worthy or not (they are). Your mindset will change as a result of the habit you've built.

I've found that the absolute best mindset to emulate is talk show host Jay Leno's. Ask yourself what Jay would do if you're struggling for what curiosity looks like and how you can wield it. Let's think about the traits he embodies in a conversation with a guest on his show.

Visualize his studio. He's got a big open space, and he is seated at a desk. His guest is seated at a chair adjacent to the desk, and it's literally like they exist in a world of their own. When Jay has a guest on his show, that guest is the center of his world for the next ten minutes. They are the most interesting person he has ever come across, everything they say is spellbinding, he is insatiably curious about their stories, and he reacts to anything they say with an uproarious laugh and otherwise exaggerated reaction that they were seeking. He is charmingly positive and can always find a humorous spin on a negative aspect of a story.

His sole purpose is to make his guest comfortable on the show, encourage them to talk about themselves, and ultimately make them feel good and look good. In turn, this makes them share revealing things they might not otherwise share and create a connection and chemistry with him that is so important for a talk show. The viewers at home can tell in an instant if either party is mailing it in or faking it, so his job literally depends on his ability to connect on a deeper level.

Even with grumpy or more quiet guests, he is able to elevate their energy levels and attitudes simply by being intensely interested in them (at an energy level slightly above theirs) and encouraging them by giving them the great reactions that they seek. It's almost as if he plays the game "How little can I say to get the most out of people?"

Of course, in your life, this equates to those people you come across that are like pulling teeth to talk to. A little bit of friendly encouragement and affirmation can make even the meekest clam open up. So acting this way is beneficial for both parties. Imagine the relief you can create at dreaded networking events. People like those who like them, so when you react the way they want, it encourages them to be more outgoing and open with you.

Jay Leno would later go on the record lamenting how often he disliked his guests and how boring he found the actors and actresses that he would be forced to speak to. But that's a testament to how highly trained his habit of curiosity was. He started by making a conscious decision to be curious, built the habit, and engaged his guests easily; do you think his guests could tell if he was interested or not? Doubtful.

Curiosity allows people to feel comfortable enough to speak freely beyond a superficial level—because you are demonstrating that you care and that you will listen when they open up. People won't be inclined to reveal their secret thoughts if they think it will be met with apathy, after all. So whether you have to fake it till you make it, Jay Leno is who your mindset and attitude should feel like.

It's a banal and often-used quote, but for good reason: Dale Carnegie said it best— "You can make more friends in two months by becoming truly interested in other people than you can in two years by trying to get other people interested in you."

In case curiosity still isn't coming naturally

to you, here are some more specific patterns of thought you can use to practice.

I wonder what they are like? When you start to wonder about the other person, it changes your perspective on them completely. You start to care about them—not only about their shallow traits, such as their occupation or how their day is going, but what motivates them and what makes them act in the way they do.

Having a sense of wonder about someone is one of the most powerful mindsets you can have because it makes you want to scratch your itch. Scratching the itch of curiosity will become secondary to everything else because you simply want to know about the other person.

Suppose you had a sense of wonder about computers as a child. You were probably irritating with how many questions you asked to anyone that seemed to have knowledge about computers.

What kind of attention span are you going to devote to computers, and what kind of questions are you going to ask? You are going to skip the small talk interview questions and get right down to the details because it's what you care and wonder about.

Keeping the mindset of wonderment will completely change the way you interact with people because you will suddenly care, and much of the time, we don't notice that we don't care about the person we are talking to. You'll dig deeper and deeper until you can put together a picture of what you are wondering about.

What can they teach me? Don't read this from the perspective of attempting to gain what you can from someone. Read it from the perspective of seeing others as being people worthy of your attention. Everyone has valuable knowledge, whether it applies to your life or not. Everyone is great at something, and everyone is a domain expert in something that you are not.

The main point is to ignite an interest in the other person as opposed to an apathetic approach. Imagine if you were a huge skiing junkie, and you met someone that used to be a professional skier. They may have even reached the Olympics in their prime.

What will follow? You'll be thrilled by what you can potentially learn and gain from the other person, and that will guide the entire interaction. Again, there will be a level of interest and engagement if you view others as worthy of talking to.

Whether we like to admit it or not, sometimes we feel some people are not worth our time. It's a bad habit, and this line of thinking is one of the first steps toward breaking it. Everyone is worth our time, but you won't be able to discover it if you don't put in the work.

What do we have in common? This is an investigation into the life experiences you share with someone. It instantly makes them more engaging and interesting— because we feel that they are more similar to us! It may sound a bit egotistical, but we are undoubtedly more captivated by people that share the same views and interests as us.

It may even *elevate* people, especially if we are surrounded by people different from us. For instance, if you discovered that a new stranger was born in the same hospital as you were, despite being in a different country, you would instantly feel more open to them. But you wouldn't have discovered that if you didn't make an attempt at communicating.

You are going to be on a hunt, and you will ask the important questions that get you where you want to be. You might jump from topic to topic, or you might dive in and ask directly.

All three of these attitudes drastically change how you approach people and, subsequently, what you talk to them about. When you have something to fixate on besides talking for talking's sake, it just becomes easier.

When you think about these attitudes to aid curiosity, there's no reason to think they aren't true. We're not always the best at everything we try our hand at, and we're not all that and a bag of chips. Other people have at least five things that they can teach us in a pinch. We also inevitably share commonalities with others, even though they may be below the surface.

Curiosity can still be hard, which is why my final suggestion for creating curiosity is to make a game of it. Your goal is to learn as much about the other person as possible. Alternatively, assume there is something extremely thrilling and exciting about the other person, and make it your quest to find it. Eventually, you'll find what you're looking for, and you'll have dug deep to do so.

Chances are, you are severely underrating the people you meet. Create a game for yourself and you'll struggle less to appear curious and interested. However difficult it is to admit, our mindsets surrounding others significantly impede our ability to connect with them. These patterns of thoughts influence our actions.

The next time you go out to a cafe or store, put these attitudes to the test with the captive audience of the baristas or cashiers you come across—the lucky few who are paid to be nice to you.

Do you perceive these workers to be below you, or do you treat them differently than you would treat a good friend? Do you have a sense of wonderment and curiosity about them? What do you think they can teach you, and what do you have in common with them?

These are levels of thought that are easy to reach if we meet someone who has a clear sense of superiority or authority, but we ignore these levels of care for everyone else.

Do you tend to ask the baristas or cashiers about their day and actually care about their answer? If not, do you think you'll be able to simply "turn it on" when you're around people you care about?

Practice your mindsets for communication. It's the easiest practice you'll have because you don't have to lift a finger. And if you realize that everything in this chapter is extremely difficult, you might have some biggcr problems to address.

Takeaways:

- Communication is tough. But it all starts with the way you think about it. It's your approach—your mindset. Only then can the tips and tactics you'll learn later be of any use. What kind of patterns of thought will benefit you in your quest for better communication and closer ties?
- First, be intentional about your communication and engagement. Relationships aren't built on luck; they're built on you taking the initiative. Every relationship needs to escape a certain threshold of interest, and often, you must find yourself making the first move.
- Second, change the goal you have when communicating with people. Too many of us are fixated on impressing people. This backfires in many ways. Instead, change your goal to engage or entertain others, which are pursuits that keep other people as the top priority.

- Third, stay curious about people. Admittedly, this is hard because we just don't feel others are always worth our time. But this, in and of itself, is a mindset to snap out of. Ask yourself what people can teach you, what is unique about people, and what similarities you have. If all else fails, make a game out of discovering people.

Chapter 2. Reading Between the Lines

Interestingly enough, the second chapter in this book on communication isn't about communication in the traditional sense of the word. That's because communication is much more than the words that we speak or hear. Studies have quoted figures from 50 to 90% that communication—the message and emotion we get from others—is based on nonverbal body language. Add that to additional communication based on subtext, context, implication, and inference, and you'll almost wonder what impact our actual words have.

Whatever the case, what we think we are communicating is often overshadowed or outright contradicted by what is meant to be interpreted between the lines. Extending on the example from the prior chapter, direct and explicit communication might be the 100 words we know in a foreign language, while we are clueless about the rest.

Accordingly, the impression and relationships we build with others are based mostly on those unspoken aspects. It's not that the words we use don't matter—they do. But the way in which we use them, and the contexts we use them in, are far more important in our overall communication.

Unfortunately, for many of us, these might as well be incantations for magic spells, based on how straightforward they seem. That's what this chapter seeks to address and rectify. And from a logical standpoint, why not tackle what makes up the majority of communication first?

What influences the snap judgments we make about people? What makes us come across someone for a split second and come away thinking:

- I just liked that person's vibe.
- They seemed like a good person.
- I had a good feeling about them.
- I don't know what it was, but I just liked them.

When you muster up the time and courage, ask five of your friends to reach into their memory banks and recall their first impression of you in the form of adjectives.

Some of your friends might say that you were exciting. Others will say you were intelligent. Even others might say that you were odd and unapproachable. Expect a list of positive adjectives and a list of not-so-positive adjectives. Presumably, you weren't aware you were acting any differently, but your actions changed depending on the context, and so did their interpretations.

After you've gotten the list of adjectives, park yourself in front of a mirror and don't say a word. Rather, demonstrate the facial expressions, tones of voice, and body language that correspond to these adjectives. You'll probably be acting in ways that are across the entire spectrum of human behavior—and that's all while you thought you were acting in a normal and consistent manner.

The point of this exercise is to begin to understand just how many ways you are communicating without moving your lips and how much is left up to interpretation—even when you feel that you've definitively presented yourself in a certain way.

One of the keys to communicating more clearly and being able to read between the lines of what people say is to understand *subtext.*

Sorting Through Subtext

Like many, Paul got a part-time job to give him extra cash as he got his university degree. He decided to work in a local electronics store because he knew the people, the area, and the product like the back of his hand. Or so he thought. Imagine his surprise when he discovered he wasn't the big sales star he made himself out to be during the interview process.

Everyone else seemed to hit their sales quotas with ease, yet there he was, stuck barely reaching the lower end of the target. What made matters worse was the fact that other staff members had absolutely no technical knowledge, yet they surpassed Paul in sales every single month.

How could that be?

Paul's sales were so bad that his boss called him in for a performance meeting to address the problem. Dave, the boss, was a smart guy—he had virtually no formal qualifications and yet here he owned his own very profitable store. Instead of pointing out where Paul went wrong, he decided to match him up with his top salesman to discover how the sales techniques differed.

For the entire afternoon, Paul tagged along with the top-performing salesperson, Sam. As Paul observed, he noticed something interesting. The customers were all completely the same, the queries were all the same, and his solutions were the same—except for one small thing.

Where Paul would give up or move on, Sam offered additional recommendations and moved in for the kill.

He realized this when a customer was looking at a camera. The customer raised his hands and declared the product to be "fine." At this point, Sam picked up a more expensive camera and walked them through its features. Paul wouldn't usually do that—when the customer said something was "fine," he would continue focusing on closing the sale on the same camera.

But to his surprise, the customer ended up buying the more expensive camera. As soon as the customer left the store, Paul asked Sam, "What made you suggest a whole new product? Isn't that just confusing the customer? I thought he said it was fine!"

Sam just laughed and said, "Just because the customer says it's fine doesn't mean it is.

Fine is not positive. It usually means they want something more or their expectations haven't been met."

Paul quickly realized the reason he was underperforming. He was taking people's words literally and only at face value, and because of that, he was missing the real messages people were sending him. Whatever was being said was the only thing Paul was operating on, and he didn't consider that communication would occur in any other way.

Sam explained that people's words were merely the tip of the iceberg in terms of what they wanted to communicate, and "fine" said with a flat speaking tone was as a good as "this sucks." That one simple statement made a huge change in Paul's sales, as he began trying to dig beneath the words themselves and pick up on the meaning behind them.

This is a textbook example of *subtext*. Subtext will help you achieve your goals, both personally and professionally, as you begin to truly respond to what people are trying to communicate. Don't be like Paul.

So what is subtext? Communication can be divided up into two categories: overt and covert. Overt is the words we say and the explicit messages we want to convey. This is when we directly tell someone that we're hungry and ask for a hamburger.

Subtext is the covert type of communication. It's almost never directly said, relies on literally anything besides the direct message coming out of someone's mouth, and requires correct interpretation. Using subtext to say "I'm hungry" would include: rubbing your stomach, licking your lips, pointing out that there is a menu on a nearby table, and mentioning that your previous meal was tiny.

Not everyone is going to pick up on those signs, but it is undeniable what the person wanted to convey. We routinely communicate through these indirect means and hope that it saves us the trouble of being direct. Subsequently, understanding the subtext under and surrounding people's seemingly benign statements gives you insight into their true feelings and thoughts.

For example, how do the overt dialogues below differ from the subtextual, covert message? Here, it's what is *not said* that completes the message. The subtext is that the question wasn't replied to in a convincing manner and, thus, is less than sincere. Suppose the answerer of the question has a history of being blunt.

"Am I fat?"
"No, you're not fat."
Translation: You might be a little bit fat.

"Am I fat?"
"No, but I suppose you could maybe lose a couple of pounds."
Translation: Yeah, you're definitely fat now.

Subtext can be delivered through vocal tone, phrasing, delivery, reference to prior experiences, knowledge of relationships, body language, gesticulation, circumstances, and even moods. It sounds abstract and confusing, but just imagine that subtext is everything we want to say besides the *exact words* we use.

In fact, that's one of the big reasons we use it. It allows us to navigate the world through indirect and nonconfrontational means. This is what made Sam such a great salesperson, as he knew customers were indirectly communicating their unhappiness, and he knew how to capitalize. If you're great at subtext, it saves time, it's efficient, and it imparts great emotional intelligence by understanding people's ever-shifting circumstances.

Subtext doesn't always exist, but becoming better at recognizing subtext will help you figure out if there is something worth paying deeper attention to in your interactions. It can be as subtle as a millisecond glance between two people to establish who will exit a door first or as overt as a dismissive hand gesture in the midst of a negotiation.

Subtext appears in every situation, from work and dating to social situations and family dynamics. You probably remember your parents being furious at you for coming home at a ridiculous hour as a student. Why were they furious? At first glance, it's because you disobeyed them and they wanted to punish you.

But what's the subtext? You were out late, and they had no way of contacting you. They might also have known that you were spending time with unsavory influences. The subtext is that they were frightened out of their minds, and anger is the way they expressed their fear. When you understand the subtext and why people are reacting in certain situations, you gain clarity into people's true feelings.

Dating is an area where subtext is prevalent. In fact, much of dating can be said to be subtext, because dating functions on sexual tension and not revealing true intentions upfront. If you ask someone to dinner and they tell you they are busy, they might be busy, or they might not be interested.

If you ask the same person out four times and each time they say they're busy, then there is additional subtext for you to read. Take the context into account and things aren't looking good for you on the romantic front.

If your supervisor assigns you less and less challenging projects while telling you that "things are slow," what do you suppose might be happening? Maybe work is slow at the moment. But what if you observe that all of your coworkers are working overtime every single day? The additional unfortunate subtext for you to read is that your supervisor doesn't think you are capable and is just putting you where you can do the least damage.

The fact is, we rely on subtext most of the time. Through our behavior and choice of words, we transmit clues and desperately hope people pick up on them. Of course, this is the origin of passive-aggressive behavior—we don't feel comfortable saying something directly, so our indirect measures become more and more aggressive and unpleasant. As a species, we are fairly avoidant and nonconfrontational. Not many people feel comfortable wearing their opinions and hearts on their sleeves, especially when it clashes with those of other people. Directness is inherently tense, so it's something we prefer to avoid.

When you're communicating with someone, it's worth asking what's driving the communication. Is it the overt spoken words or the covert message to be transmitted by subtext? Is there additional subtext to decipher, and if there is, what does it mean?

A helpful method to imagine how subtext works in social situations is to imagine how it factors into a novel or a screenplay. When you're watching a movie or reading a book, you don't usually get told what the characters understand, feel, or think, and despite that, you come away with a clear sense of meaning about the scenes and relationships. This is all because of subtext.

In this context, it's commonly referred to as what is under the skin of the character—what drives and motivates them, what they feel toward everyone else in the story, and what's under the surface of all of their actions. Without giving characters clear motivations and having everyone in the movie operate only on a "what you see is what you get" level, you end up with a flat movie with no emotional impact.

Even in movies, there can be ambiguity in the subtext—sometimes intentional and sometimes not. This is the part the audience must fill in, which is why two people can come out of a film and have radically different ideas about the meaning the director was trying to convey.

Let's take a look at an example scene in detail to illustrate this clearly. Always remember that we have to separate the covert and overt communication.

Imagine a room where a man clasps a tiny baby blue box in his hands. The table is decorated with roses and champagne. A woman appears at the side of the frame and prepares to leave the room. She does not notice the man in the corner. He says, "Wait!"

Why does the man call the woman?

If you say, "Because he wants to propose to

her," you have understood the subtext present in this basic scene. The dialogue never says that the man wants to propose marriage to the woman. You inferred that from a combination of the mood, description, and the scene itself.

Is the word "wait" subtext? In this scene, the man is telling the woman to stop. There is nothing hidden in his words, other than "Don't go!" or perhaps "Stay!" depending on how the word is delivered.

Imagine instead that the man overtly says, "I have a table laid out here for you and I intend to propose with this beautiful ring I bought from Tiffany & Co." It's not something that would happen in real life, and thus, movies have to be written with subtext that allows people to understand what's happening.

Filling in the details of any incoming communication through subtext is integral to understanding people. Aside from that, you'll understand that people sometimes mistakenly assume the presence of subtext when there is none and, conversely, that you mistakenly assume that your intentional subtext is always received. No two people have the same set of experiences and biases to perfectly match subtext interpretations, but there are clear elements to look for to improve upon this skill.

Knowing the significance of subtext to better communication, you can begin to identify subtext to better understand people. If you look closely, you will soon find that almost everything a person says has shades of subtext meant to consciously or unconsciously communicate additional messages.

Pay attention to someone's prior history and experiences and how they might relate to the current situation. It colors their entire perspective, priorities, and motivations. For example, if you ask a divorcee about their opinion of marriage, a quick evaluation of their history will help you come to realize that their advice might be negatively biased—if not overtly, at least covertly. They may say that "marriage is a decision to be made for every individual couple," but that's less than a ringing endorsement. It makes that neutral statement take a definite negative tone.

If you know someone's general personality traits, you can often make a call by analyzing the situation from a neutral perspective. If someone is extremely meek and quiet and says something to the effect of "I agree... I suppose," then it probably means they are internally screaming "NO!" Essentially, consider the source and how a person's experiences color their communication.

Judge someone's authenticity by analyzing the tone of their voice. Are they angry, serious, or sarcastic? Does the tone match the message? If someone says yes, but they use a sarcastic tone, then they probably mean no. If someone says yes, but they are angry, then they are probably not happy with the outcome. If they are serious and they say yes, then they are conflicted or they probably don't care. There is a virtually unlimited amount of interpretations of vocal tone, but most of them indeed mean that the words aren't meant to be taken at face value.

Pay attention to eye contact. Keep track of a speaker's eye contact as they deliver a message to you. Direct eye contact is always the best and might represent truthfulness, but too much eye contact might represent extreme focus for lying. If someone's eyes are to the roof, it is a sign they are thinking about something else or they are ignoring you or they are simply bored. If their eyes are to the floor, they may be avoiding you, feeling sad, or even concealing the truth. Whenever anyone is giving you too much eye contact or avoiding eye contact altogether, it's a good time to start looking for further clues to make a thorough judgment.

Keep a close watch on body language and gestures that may change the meaning of words. Crossed arms are famous at signaling disagreement, dismissive hand gestures show your ideas are being rejected, while active hand gestures could mean they agree with what you say. When people are in sync with you, they often mirror your body language.

Observe how people respond to you. When you look at how patient people are, how nice they act, and how accommodating they try to be, you can gauge how they feel about what you say. This also extends to how much silence you hear and how much interest they show. If someone takes two beats to answer a simple question, they had to think about their reply and may be using subtext to communicate negativity even if they agree with you.

Another aspect to consider, which may require more intense observational skills, is to see how much they deviate from their usual pattern of behavior. If your supervisor is typically upbeat, what does it mean that they are somber and negative? It can turn a proclamation of "Things are going well..." into the exact opposite message.

Subtext leaves clues that you can harness to become an expert communicator. People leave signs everywhere. Awareness of this will help you achieve your goals and get you to where you want to be both professionally and personally, as you know not only how to get what you want but also how to give others what they need to facilitate your success.

Of course, the tough part is deciphering these aspects of people simultaneously and instantly, as you might do in a normal everyday conversation. You might be able to train yourself to pick up on specific types of subtext and social cues, but can you pick up on them while trying to find others? Or will you only be able to observe so many things at once? It might seem like you'd need three brains and six pairs of eyes to pick up on so many things at once—at the beginning, this might be true.

But the only thing we can do is start small and train yourself until these things become a subconscious habit to consider—*why did they say that and what could it mean from them?*

We mentioned social cues earlier—they are specific types of subtext that are relatively universal and don't depend on individual traits and experiences. Social cues are the message we really want to send but would rather not say directly.

As with subtext, if you lack an understanding of specific social cues, it means you are probably missing half of the overall message people are sending you. As mentioned, we rely heavily on subtext to do our dirty work for us. Accordingly, most social cues send the message of when people are interested in you or not. Yes or no, essentially.

If someone keeps talking and engaging with you but their body starts to turn away, what is the overall message they are trying to send? They might say, "It's so great to see you!" but their body is saying otherwise. Clearly, they are uninterested in continuing the interaction, but that's just not something you want to outright say in respect to social norms and courtesy.

Despite what people's words are or how interested they appear to be, what direction is their body pointing or moving in? If someone's toes or shoulders are square to you, that's a good indication they are actually interested in you and not seeking an escape from you (in the direction their toes or shoulders are pointed). However, if they are actively moving away and increasing the distance from you, there aren't many other ways to interpret that: they want to get away from you, politely.

These cues aren't easy to catch because they occur simultaneous to what appears to be a normal conversation. This means you actually have two tasks: (1) processing the conversation and responding appropriately and (2) being on the lookout for social cues.

Similarly, if you are sitting with someone and they seem eager to stand up or otherwise get into motion, it's a cue they probably want to leave. Or if you are at their office, cubicle, or home, it might mean they wish for *you* to leave. They are hoping you will follow their lead and stand up as well. This is also what happens when we look at our watches in front of people—in the hopes that they recognize that we want to move on with our day.

Another situation where you'll see this

behavior is when people start to become preoccupied with something else when they are talking to you, such as reading a book or putting on headphones and listening to music. In hindsight, these are all very clear signs of disinterest, but we don't always realize their meaning in the moment.

Another social cue to be more aware of is when people are interested or not in what you have to say. If someone gives you a short, one-word answer, they are not interested in continuing that line of conversing. They might not even be interested in continuing the interaction with you overall.

If there is a slightly extended silence, a silence longer than either party grasping for something to say can stand, they are not interested in continuing that conversation. They have *let* that silence come and stay to discourage further interaction. It's an odd notion that people may intentionally make their conversations bad, but remember, they are using it to send a message by subtext that they aren't interested in continuing.

A pause is not always an invitation for you to fill the silence. If you find that you are engaging in a monologue, the other person has likely tuned out and is nodding their head and smiling out of courtesy while screaming inside. We've all had the experience of being trapped in a room by an overly talkative coworker, supervisor, or other person we don't want to refuse. They are the ones who miss the social cue of silence as a sign for leaving.

Remember, social cues say what people actually intend. These are things we can see that just require a bit of forethought to understand people better.

We can also look at general physical movements and body language clues. In the field of poker, bluffing, or lying about your cards, is a common way to win. However, most people possess what are known as "tells," which are subconscious bodily movements and tics that give away the fact that they are lying. Of course, these "tells" can also function as social cues—if someone does not feel aligned with the words they are using, they might be giving it away with their body language and movement. For instance: if they say, "I'm so happy to see you!" while slowly backing away from you and crossing their arms.

Subtext, at the very least, should teach us that there is almost always more than meets the eye when it comes to communication. The more you realize how much we depend on subtext to communicate even very simple things, the more you'll realize how much you've missed about people in the past.

I want to end the section on subtext with a small exercise to get you into the mood. It's fairly easy: go out into public and observe people interacting—for example, sitting at a café and covertly watching the people at nearby tables. You can't hear the overt conversation, so you're going to make a guess at the subtext of the covert communication. Assign backstories, emotions, and motivations to the people you are observing. Go out on a limb and make up stories. Once you get better at subtext, you'll find that the stories you create in situations like this will become more and more accurate.

In the greater scheme of things, subtext is part of simply being more and empathetic. We already know that humans love to communicate through subtext, for better or worse. It's just not in our nature to be direct and potentially confrontational—perhaps that's an instinctual defensive measure. After all, the fewer confrontations, the better chance of survival.

When you gain the skill of empathy, you no longer have to go through the arduous process of analyzing subtext and trying to figure out what people are trying to say. When you have trained empathy, you know what they are thinking before they even say it. It's because you know what emotions they are likely feeling.

Empathy is the ability to understand the feelings of other people. Some take it further and define empathy as the ability to share emotions with others, but that's not always necessary to use empathy in daily communication. Just knowing is enough—

it's the ability to walk a mile in someone else's shoes to withhold judgment, understand better, and communicate like you're reading their minds.

Most people have empathy, but it only comes in spurts or it doesn't go very deep into feeling what other people feel. We might be impacted for a split second when we see a homeless person, but as soon as we walk past them, we tend to immediately forget about them. Out of sight, out of mind.

It's not to say that you should put all your obligations to the side and fully commiserate with the plights of the world à la Mother Teresa, but there is certainly room for greater empathy in the pursuit of better communication. A key to empathy concerns judgment; when it comes first in the form of a snapshot, without considering wider context and intentions, empathy is doomed to fail. I would suggest a five-step thinking process that comes courtesy of *The Avatar Journal*, an online publication focused on compassion and empathy. Remember, the purpose is to not take people at face value and to try to understand their latent emotions.

Step 1: "Just like me, this person is seeking happiness in his/her life."

Step 2: "Just like me, this person is trying to avoid suffering in his/her life."

Step 3: "Just like me, this person has known sadness, loneliness, and despair."

Step 4: "Just like me, this person is seeking to fill his/her needs."

Step 5: "Just like me, this person is learning about life."

Take the example of the homeless person you see on the streets. How might going through this five-step thought process put them in a new light about their struggles and daily realities? How might you view them differently and understand their lives a bit more?

We are always choosing our interpretations of people, whether consciously or subconsciously. When you engage in empathy, you make the choice to interpret them with psychological closeness—as if they were an extension of you. You begin to take on their views and thoughts without really trying, and that's quite an efficient means of reading between the lines to improve your communication.

Takeaways:

- Communication really is not about the words coming out of our mouths. For better or worse, we really communicate through indirect means. Perhaps this was an evolutionary reaction to avoiding confrontation or developing social skills; whatever the case, we need to learn to read between the lines to communicate effectively.
- A large piece of that puzzle is to understand subtext. What is subtext? It's taking into account everything *except* the explicit words that are spoken—the words are overt, whereas subtext is an overt communication. It's looking at context, personal history, tone of voice, body language, and delivery to interpret

a message that could very well be the complete opposite from the explicit words you hear. Just imagine how you tend to understand the motivations and intentions of movie and book characters without them directly saying or thinking it.

- Specific pieces of subtext that are relatively universal are social cues. For our purposes, some of the most useful cues are about people's interest or lack thereof. Look at people's general responsiveness, chattiness, silence, and body positioning.

- Empathy is the final piece of reading between the lines. In a sense, it prevents you from having to do so, because when you think in terms of empathy, you innately understand people's emotions and thoughts. This allows you to know what people are thinking without having to necessarily analyze subtext or take context into account. You can achieve this by focusing on a five-step thought process that humanizes the other person and makes them more relatable.

Chapter 3. Good Vibrations

The next time you find yourself among a group of people, you will notice that there is at least one person that everybody tends to gravitate toward. There's just something about that one person that attracts attention and creates respect.

The reason one person tends to become the center of attention is because, more often than not, they radiate positivity. That person makes people feel good about themselves. That person contributes something to the atmosphere that makes people feel welcomed, appreciated, and comfortable. It's no surprise that people want to be around people like this.

They're not the life of the party, and they're

not the most charming people, but there is something that makes people want to be around them. It seems like they have the superpower of being magnetic. But in reality, it's much simpler than that.

At our core, we are mere animals that succumb to positive conditioning. If someone makes us feel good, shows interest in us, and compliments us, we want to be around them. Some people can do this with baked goods; others can do this with their positivity. You can do it, too, in many simple and subtle ways. Remember, we learned earlier that we should realign our goals to focus on other people. Instead of trying to show ourselves in a certain light, we should try to create an enjoyable experience for others. This chapter takes this notion to the next level.

The first way to tailor your communication to create good vibrations is to become proficient and liberal with compliments.

Compliments

You might think it difficult to compliment

somebody you've just met. It may feel awkward and uncomfortable. You might even feel that you can't think of anything to compliment random people on. But all of those assumptions are wrong.

If you think about it, you probably have positive thoughts or observations about people running through your head all day, so there's no reason not to simply give voice to them. We just tend to fixate on sneer-worthy aspects more than we like. Our judgmental voices are far louder than our praising voices.

Whatever the case, beginning to think in terms of positivity toward others will transform the way you communicate. You don't need to be funny or charming to create positivity in others.

Within the world of compliments, there are two levels I want to differentiate between. The first level is the low-hanging fruit— there are only so many times someone can hear that they have nice eyes and still be impacted by it. This level is what most people are stuck on. They are more likely to be simple observations rather than in-depth statements. You'll know the difference between the two levels of compliments by the impact it has on the person. Eyes are great—but it's something rather shallow to point out.

The second level of compliment goes below the surface. For maximum impact, compliment people for two things (besides the obvious and superficial). Compliment people on (1) things they have control over and (2) things they have made a conscious choice about. There may be significant overlap between the two.

For instance, no one has control over the color of their eyes; thus, it's not a very impactful compliment. However, someone has made a very conscious choice to wear a specific hairstyle that takes an hour to get ready. Other examples include specific habits, specific words and phrases people use, distinct fashion sense, unique thoughts, and so on.

Why are these aspects so much more personal and impactful to compliment? It's because they reflect the person's thought processes and identity. These are choices people consciously make to represent themselves—their tastes and values. They don't do it for others, but they are hoping to be judged positively and lauded for their choices. The more outrageous something might be, the more valuable positive confirmation is. Therefore, when you compliment someone on their choices and thoughts, you validate them to the highest degree.

Compliment things that they've obviously put some thought into. This might include a bright shirt, a distinctive handbag, an unusual piece of art, or a vintage car. These things are out of the ordinary and uncommon and reflect a deliberate deviation from the norm. You never know if someone's persona is ingrained in the fact that they choose to wear Hawaiian shirts. By complimenting someone on something they've clearly chosen with purpose, you acknowledge and validate the statement they have chosen to make about themselves.

Other things you can compliment people on that show individual choice are their manners, the way they phrase certain ideas, their opinions, their worldviews, and their perspectives. In this way, compliments act more as validation versus merely pointing out something positive.

People aren't really complimented that much on a daily basis—especially men. We can easily see this because of the amount of awkward fumbling most people engage in when receiving a genuine compliment. Make it a goal to see people fumble about the compliments you give them—the more fumbling, the greater the impact you've made.

As you can see, the best compliments require a measure of attention and focus that you probably aren't used to. If you're really studying and analyzing someone—not just physically—then your lines of communication will be that much stronger.

Give, Give, Give

The next part of creating positivity and

good vibrations is to become a giver. This is probably a lesson you learned when you were a child (sharing is caring), but adulthood has beaten that out of you. It's time to bring it back to the basics. Giving is a cornerstone of what people want to spend time with. It might mean that we are affected by simple incentives, but like complimenting, if you begin thinking in terms of how other people benefit, the way you interact with others will fundamentally change.

According to Adam Grant, professor at the Wharton School of Business at the University of Pennsylvania, there are three types of people in relationships:

1. Takers
2. Matchers
3. Givers

Takers view relationships as a competition and seek to extract everything they can for themselves. They will take as much as possible while giving as little as possible. Hopefully, a taker in your life is acting without self-awareness, driven by their self-centeredness. But that's not always the case. Relationships are a means to an end for them. "I have to look out for myself because no one else will."

Matchers seek to balance giving and taking. They are concerned with feelings of fairness and equality and grow uncomfortable when one party gives too much or too little. There is some expectation of equality, even if it is unspoken. Nothing quite comes for free, but they are not stingy or selfish. "I have no problem with that as long as it's fair."

Givers are the definition of altruism. They are the opposite of takers and seek to give and provide as much as possible with little regard for themselves. As long as they are safe and secure, they will keep giving for as long as they can. There is zero expectation for reciprocation, and sometimes they are selfless to a fault. "As soon as everyone else eats, I can eat."

Which of these three types do you think people are most interested in connecting with? This section has focused on the small ways you can become a giver in your everyday life and how it helps your communication efforts. It doesn't take much effort or time.

Thankfully, giving comes in many forms, so it's not about having money or the ability to buy gifts. Giving is about the positive emotions you can give people. If you can do something for someone or make them feel a way they want to feel, you've given successfully and will be held in high esteem.

Everyone has needs and desires, and we are usually ignorant or passive to them. Giving is about being proactive to these needs and desires—you have them, too, so it shouldn't be so difficult to decipher what other people want.

Get into the habit of thinking how you can proactively help a person to fulfill their needs or desires, both practical, like at work, and emotional, like making them feel good about themselves. People's needs or desires can be primary, what you can see obviously on the surface, or they can be far more profound and deep—what is below the surface and emotional or psychological in nature.

In the current moment, is there a need or desire someone might have that you can assist with? Probably. Needs are generally things you can provide that prevent people from feeling a negative emotion, while desires are things you can provide to cause people to feel a positive emotion. It's a matter of simply getting into the habit.

An example of meeting someone's practical need or desire is helping someone who needs a ride to work. You can provide the ride yourself or you can help them make arrangements for transportation. Because of you, they are able to keep their livelihood. If they have just eaten a greasy hamburger, you might grab them a couple of napkins. If you realize that they haven't eaten lunch, ask if they are hungry or recommend them a restaurant.

An emotional or psychological need or desire is more complex. But just understand that everyone wants to feel loved, respected, and worth something in this world. There are universal themes in what keep us in a good mood versus a bad mood. If you see someone is eating lunch alone at work, this person may be feeling lonely and left out. He or she may feel alienated by coworkers or may be in need of emotional support at the moment. You can make a tremendous difference by asking, "Do you want to join me for lunch?" Reach out to this person and make him or her feel wanted and accepted and fulfill the human desire for company and support.

Now, you can't reasonably spend your whole life serving others, so look for five-minute favors—things you can do in five minutes or less. For example, you can open a door for someone who is struggling with carrying a big box or you can offer someone a ride on your way to work. Listen to someone for a short amount of time. Shoot someone who is having a rough day a positive text. Think about proactive ways you can help people out that require little effort and investment on your part. You can make a big difference to others without cutting into your own time and needs.

They may be quick to you, but the value of

the gesture will be immense and you will cement yourself as the type of person that provides positive value with your presence alone.

You don't have to offer help only when people ask for it; most people never ask for help because they are embarrassed and don't want to inconvenience others. You relieve people of the embarrassment of asking, most people's biggest obstacle, and make people's lives easier. Being intuitive makes you more compassionate and likable in general. There doesn't have to be a manipulative stigma attached to giving; you just have to understand that humans are naturally selfish and naturally gravitate toward those who can help us.

Beyond being helpful, there are a number of ways you can actively add value to people's lives, even passively.

Connect people. Try to be a connector and proactively introduce people for mutually beneficial relationships. If someone needs or desires something, it's not too hard to think of someone who could help out directly or indirectly. As usual, the gesture is worth just as much as the actual connection. Strive to be the person who knows what everyone is good at and can help people make things happen. Your value in this instance is the promise of beneficial connections. There's a reason we hang around with VIPs we don't enjoy personally—because we know we might benefit in some way from being in their presence.

Be the planner. Take on the role of the planner. If you volunteer, it's doubtful anyone will fight you for the privilege since it can often be a hassle. However, your value is actually quite high here. People will begin to look at you and depend on you to make things happen—it quickly becomes a position of leadership and power. Organize get-togethers. Help someone conceive a bachelor party. Plan a vacation for a group, or rent out a room and throw a party. People will like you because you do the hard part and can be relied on for social gatherings and bringing happiness into people's lives.

Be entertaining. Recall that giving isn't limited to things with monetary value; giving is about addressing people's needs or desires to create positive feelings. Therefore, giving can be entertainment as well. In fact, it's one of the forms of value that most influence everyday friendships and relationships. You may not see eye to eye politically with your best friend, and they may borrow money from you constantly and never pay you back, but if they make you laugh and are fun to be around, their relative value is great enough for you to continue spending time with them.

Indeed, most friendships are formed simply because people enjoy being around each other. That is value in its purest form—if I spend time with someone and know I will be happy and laugh, I will gravitate toward them. This can take the form of compelling conversation, captivating anecdotes, humorous observations, or jokes. You don't have to be the life of the party; being entertained is a purely subjective matter.

Everyone likes different types of movies,

and movies are almost always preferred to dry lectures—because they are entertaining. Thus, entertainment as value makes you magnetic.

Entertain people by focusing on them, their interests, and their lives. Entertain people by understanding and being familiar with current events so you can have an engaging and thoughtful dialogue. Further entertain them by being understanding of different histories and cultures so you can add context into any conversation. Entertain people by giving knowledge they seek or soliciting knowledge from them and thrusting them into the pleasing role of a teacher. Entertain by being more spontaneous, asking people hypothetical questions, and being less predictable.

Providing value to people by being entertaining is actually advice about how to be a better conversationalist in disguise, isn't it? It diverges from typical conversation advice because it takes you out of the equation and asks you to focus on others and how you can prioritize their needs. When you realize that successful relationships don't begin with focusing on you, and instead should be weighted toward others, it necessarily requires that you have a different approach.

Just strive to leave someone in a better condition than when you found them. After every interaction, ask yourself, "Did I leave this person in a better condition than I found them? Did I uplift, inspire, and empower them? Did I cheer them up? Did I make them laugh? Did I give some love and support?"

If you approach communication with this simple intention, you will always know what to do and how to create feelings of trust and comfort.

A good example may be to cheer up a person who looks sad. Maybe your coworker comes in looking like she had a really rough day before her shift. Ask her what's wrong and try to comfort her. Bring her favorite lunch, just to get a smile out of her. You might be the only person who takes any action to make her feel better. She will notice this, and she will appreciate it.

Remember, all you wanted to do was leave this person in a better condition than before your interaction. This can be as easy as making them smile or laugh, but the point is, it's completely focused on them. If you keep in mind this intention of making people's day, it becomes crystal clear how to act to be more likable as a human being.

There's one final layer here—we all have different ways that we like to be focused on. According to researcher and author Gary Chapman, there are five love languages.

A love language, according to Chapman, is how we demonstrate or process love and affection from others. It's how you prefer to show someone that you care about them, and it's the signs you would most enjoy seeing from others that let you know they care about you as well.

For example, some people might really enjoy receiving flowers. It makes them feel loved. They don't care about expensive gifts or if their significant other stands in line for hours to buy a new gadget for them. They simply want flowers. They can appreciate the other gestures, but the flowers make them feel the most loved.

If you've ever felt unappreciated or ignored by a significant other, you might be able to point to having different love languages. We'll dive into each of the love languages in detail, and you'll be able to see that, if you don't have matching languages, then it's similar to telling someone "I love you" in French when they only speak Russian. The message is missed, which means it won't have the impact you want, if any.

The point is to take your giving habit to the next level by understanding that there are five ways to create feelings of goodwill. The five love languages and ways people process your generosity are:

1. Words of affirmation
2. Physical touch
3. Giving gifts
4. Quality time
5. Acts of service

Words of affirmation is a verbal love

language. You say it. You think out loud and make sure to acknowledge anything positive about the other person. You can compliment and praise to let them know you appreciate them. This means a small word or phrase here or there has a big impact and is a strong sign of motivation for people.

Physical touch may be more appropriate with romantic partners and close friends, but if you're a stranger, it doesn't change someone's love language. There are still ways to utilize physical touch—a pat on the shoulder, a grab of the arm, or a high five. These people use the sensation of touch as a way to feel validation and affirmation. They can feel untethered and lost without it. See how the people you meet respond to a handshake and escalate from there.

Gift giving is a simple love language. Some measure emotional interest by the gifts they receive. Of course, this person also reciprocates emotional bonding by giving gifts in return.

It's easy to think that this person is

materialistic, but those with this love language don't focus on the value of the gift. Instead, they focus on the thought and consideration behind the gift. If someone gives a gift, they were thinking about the person. The monetary value doesn't matter; it's the fact you took the effort to bring anything that matters. Keep small gifts handy, such as gum, mints, or cigarettes. Be generous with small foodstuffs like donuts. Make it a rule to never show up empty-handed, even if it's a one-dollar trinket. These are all gifts.

Quality time is when you spend uninterrupted, focused time with someone. You're completely present and you are mentally and emotionally engaged. You're not just in the same room as them. You need to differentiate between time together and quality time. The quality of the time is more important than the quantity of the time. For our purposes, it's about giving people your undivided attention.

The fifth love language and manner of serving others is acts of service.

What is an act of service? It's when you perform something for someone that makes their life easier—for example, doing the dishes for them, giving them a massage, or helping them move apartments. Regardless of what you do, these small acts of going beyond and taking care of the needs of somebody else mean a lot to them. It shows them that you actually care.

Anyone can say they support you, but if you can't see the support in terms of their actions, their words are meaningless to you. It's the small acts that really bring home the point that this person is in it with you and can go all the way. Actions speak louder than words.

This is the love language that ties in most closely with being helpful and giving in a conventional sense. It's a skill to be able look at a situation and see where you can help out.

- Can you bring someone a napkin or help them with their chair?
- Can you make space for someone at your

table?

- Can you let someone cut in line if they only have a couple of items?
- Can you hold the door for a line of people?
- Can you help someone with their jacket?

Understanding the different love languages and seeing how you can serve others in small ways will train you to look at people in fundamentally different ways. You will be looking for where and how people struggle and how you can improve their situations for them. You will be diagnosing where you can step in with generosity and care. There is a fabulous benefit to you because this is possible at little to no cost for you. So why not?

The world is filled with selfish, self-centered people. Gradually, that has become the rule, not the expectation, whenever we meet new people. Become a breath of fresh air for people by prioritizing giving, and see how this externally focused approach can elevate you instantly in people's   eyes.

Safety and Comfort

The final aspect about creating good vibrations is to allow people to feel comfortable and safe with you. The previous points were about imparting positivity, but actually, this last point will be about minimizing negativity. People just need to feel like they can be themselves around you. For instance, do people feel like they can be themselves next to a wild bear? No, they will be tense and uncomfortable because there is a sense of unpredictability and imminent danger. People feel like they can be themselves next to a fuzzy white bunny rabbit.

The lowest-hanging fruit for us to start with is feelings of negativity and how to cope with them.

We all feel negative emotions. The difference between someone who is likable and someone who is not is how we deal with these emotions. Whatever the circumstances, if you are outwardly angry, sullen, or irritable, people will avoid you in the fear that you will be their next target. That's the feeling of lack of safety. People won't feel comfortable being themselves around you if you are constantly upset, overly critical, hateful, or volatile.

This isn't about hiding your emotions necessarily, or even faking them, but if our goal is making people feel comfortable around us, you can't be a ticking time bomb that people won't feel comfortable around because they don't know when you will blow up. It's like being around someone throwing a tantrum or not handling conflict well. You have to manage your negative emotions in a way where you can still express yourself but not send people running for shelter. People have to know that whatever happens to you *stays with you* and you won't punish others for something they were not involved in.

First, be nice whenever negativity occurs. Sounds simple enough. The situation is likely tense enough that you shouldn't be making it worse by injecting your emotions into it. Don't shoot the messenger, and understand that a small bit of negativity can go a long way.

When someone is wrong, don't rub it in his or her face. It is unnecessary and only serves your ego. Making someone feel wrong in front of people causes unnecessary tension and strife. The person you humiliate will forever resent you. In the same vein, avoid criticizing someone too much and acting like you are better than them or pointing out their flaws or mistakes around others. Criticism hits hard, so you should use only the bare minimum to make your point understood.

When you are right and someone else is wrong, give that individual a face-saving way to carry out your wishes with a minimum of embarrassment and humiliation. Instead of asserting your right to be right, ask people for their advice on the next steps to rectify mistakes. That allows them to be part of the decision-making process and not just the butt of a joke. Make them feel safe to be wrong and show flaws around you.

When it comes to you being in the wrong, it

has the potential to go just as badly. This typically happens when you become defensive when receiving criticism. This is your ego and sense of pride at work. Try to be gracious about it, apologize if necessary, and listen rather than defend. Again, you want to make people feel safe in bringing you their unfiltered thoughts, even if that paints you in a negative light.

Don't take out your negative feelings like anger, jealousy, sullenness, or resentment on others. Feel them and express them, but the difference is that you shouldn't allow them to affect how you interact with others in any way. You want to minimize the negative emotions you project because your feelings are not anyone else's problem. If you are in a poor mood, don't act in a way that puts others into the same mood.

The easiest way to minimize these feelings is to divert them. Let go of thoughts that hurt you, because when you think negative thoughts, you can't help but fixate and you lower your own mood. If even for a second, your feelings flash across your face, even if you don't intend for them to. So limit the bad thinking and think more positive thoughts. Focus on what is good in life and what you are grateful for. Everyone faces hardships in life, yet some people are still lovable and a joy to be around when they are at their lowest moments.

This is because they can manage their negative emotions effectively and even productively. To harp on the same theme, you want to impart feelings of safety that people can be negative with you. If we can assume that 50% of the world's topics are negative by nature, this opens up a whole range of topics and emotions that people can explore with you.

Again, of course bad events will have a negative effect on you. It is naïve to assume that you won't ever be hurt or disturbed by the bad things that can happen in life. Feel your emotions and express them, but don't have them affect your interactions or take your emotions out on others. You will creep people out if you have no normal reactions to life. For example, if you were to lose your job, you want to act sad and let your grief or horror show.

Negative emotion management makes people feel safe around you and feel confident that you aren't going to attack. It makes you predictable in a good way—where people know they can expect only positivity from you and that you are someone they can turn to for support and cheer. In this way, you can become more reliable and dependable for people, and that's always quite likable.

The second part of making people feel safe is to tone down your judgmental tendencies.

Humans are naturally judgmental. You look at someone and you immediately form an idea about who that person is and whether or not you like that person. When someone does something, you automatically form an opinion. But being judgmental only pushes people away, at least if you express your judgment. Even if you're just judging others in front of people, who knows when you'll turn your sights onto them for judgment! Rather than pushing people away, be open-minded with the Japanese concept of *wabi sabi.*

While this term has no direct translation from Japanese into English, it's a term for what makes people who they are. *Wabi* is the quirks and glitches that people possess that separate them from everyone else. For example, someone might never match their socks. That is a unique personality identifier because it is an anomaly. *Sabi* is the inherent beauty of an individual that grows with life experience. Think of how beautiful an old man is as he shares a plethora of stories from a time way before you were born, gracing you with knowledge that you never previously had about that era of history. Therefore, together, *wabi sabi* is about enjoying and cherishing imperfections.

The roots of *wabi sabi* can be traced to ancient Buddhist teachings, where embracing imperfection is seen as the first step to achieving enlightenment, or *satori.* Seeing into yourself and into others and just accepting what you see without trying to change it is the ultimate form of enlightenment. It's also a good way to become likable.

An example of using this concept in real life might be trying to get to know a homeless man's story and trying to empathize with him instead of judging him for being dirty and assuming that he is on the streets by his own fault. Or it might be accepting it when your friend makes a silly decision and being there for your friend through the fallout, rather than judging your friend and expressing your disappointment. See a flaw or unwise decision you might judge and understand instead that it is a facet of *wabi sabi* and people are just trying their best each day.

After all, an Austrian robotics study called "To Err Is Robot: How Humans Assess and Act Toward an Erroneous Social Robot" found that people related more to robots that have their own unique flaws and quirks rather than to perfect robots without flaws. It illustrates how quirks define and make up one's personality, making a person relatable and ultimately likable. Getting to know and accepting one's quirks makes you get along with the person better. No human is perfect, so learn to embrace their imperfections as part of what makes them unique.

We never have full information on someone's decisions, and if we assume that everyone is trying the best with what they have, your judgmental tendencies will relax. If you can successfully manage negative emotions and your impulse to lash out, safety and comfort are possible. They all form the picture of the person from the beginning of the chapter—magnetic because of his or her positivity.

Takeaways:

- Sometimes the best method of communication isn't about the words themselves; it's about the feelings you create in others. To that end, positivity and good vibrations are important to open and clear lines for rapport.
- Compliments are the first way to create positivity and goodwill. They take less effort than you might expect, and it sometimes just requires thinking out loud. There are two levels of

compliments: superficial observations and ones that create a deeper impact based on people's conscious choices.

- Another way to create positivity is to become a giver. Giving is about getting into the habit of anticipating the needs and desires of other people. However, just stick to five-minute favors. Overall, ask yourself if you can leave the other person in a better condition than you found them. Once you make that your intention, you will begin to approach people differently.

- The final layer of giving is to understand the five love languages, which are particular methods of giving and showing your attention and care. The languages are words of affirmation, physical touch, giving gifts, quality time, and acts of service.

- The final aspect of creating positivity is to manage your negative emotions. This is difficult—one of the most difficult tasks for a human. But the act of biting your tongue more can make people feel safer and more comfortable around you, rather than avoiding you like a ticking time bomb. You must also seek to quell your judgmental tendencies, because otherwise people will associate you with negative feelings.

Chapter 4. Validation and Respect

This chapter is about validation, the verbal affirmation and acceptance of the emotions and viewpoints of someone we're communicating with. Validation might seem like a fairly simple concept of nodding and saying yes when people want you to, but even though it sounds relatively uncomplicated, there are right and wrong ways to validate.

I once knew a couple who had a colorful history together. They were well-liked in their social circles. One was a musician who was trying to become a songwriter. They'd had a very religious upbringing. Even though this person was an acclaimed talent to everyone they knew, their parents couldn't care less. They thought personal expression was a waste of time. Their parents would literally make fun of the songs they'd written. It was a big incentive for them to move out of the house.

The other partner, who was an office worker, experienced the same kind of invalidation from their family, although religion didn't have anything to do with it. Their parents, more or less, couldn't be bothered to care what was happening in that person's life. Nothing their child did seemed to impress them much.

Maybe that common history brought them together, and for a while they seemed to be sympathetic to each other's needs. But between them, cracks started to show. The office worker invalidated everything about the musician—their songs, their choice of music, their appearance, their own friends, and their reactions to every single emotion they showed. They'd cut down their feelings. In time, the musician stopped sharing anything of a personal nature, until one point where the frustration had gotten so unbearable that they tore the office worker down in a torrent of accusations.

The office worker and I fell out of contact, but I reconnected with the musician online a few years ago. They said they'd given up a career in music long ago. Anytime they dared to make a move, they were reminded how "incorrect" they'd been told they were, first by their parents and then by their partner. "Those things build up," they told me. "If you're brought up with the premise that nothing about you is special and the need for validation is stupid, it just takes a whole lot of incentive away. That frustrates anyone now who tries to get close to me."

My friend's story explains the importance of validation in a nutshell and how it affects much more than our immediate experience with others. It's not only saying yes and nodding at the appropriate time; its importance shows itself throughout our lives: a parent who encourages their child to express himself, a friend who listens intently about a problem they're having, or a partner who appreciates their spouse's work effort and goals.

Validation is one of the more powerful give-and-take practices of communication because it establishes respect between two people, old friend or stranger. Shutting down someone's feelings—even if they're repellant to us—effectively closes those floodgates off and isolates *both* sides of the exchange, putting the relationship at risk.

Genuine validation, on the other hand, helps everybody in the communication process score a win. The receiver gets a confirmation of their humanity, but the giver also enriches their own stature and enhances their self-worth. Generosity, trust, and eagerness to confide emerge, and communication rarely goes wrong when all those elements are working.

The Importance of Validation

Three studies, summarized in a 2010 study from the University of Rochester, highlighted the positive and subtle effects the act of validation has in a successful relationship. It's not just a way of paying attention to people or showing respect for people's wishes. That is the lowest-hanging fruit that needs to be picked, but true validation goes far deeper in making people feel embraced and heard.

In one study, researchers asked a group of undergraduates to think about someone with whom they had a significant relationship and were likely to be in contact with on a regular basis. The students maintained daily diaries in which they wrote about the best thing that happened to them on each given day. They also wrote down whether they told their friend or loved one about what they'd experienced and what their response was. The students were questioned about their feelings of kindness and generosity for the friends they spoke with.

After two weeks of this experience, researchers asked the undergraduates to reflect upon the positive events they told their friends about. Nearly unanimously, the students' feelings about their positive events were even better than when they first experienced them. Furthermore, their feelings about their loved ones also increased—based on their validations from them, they felt more inclined to express kindness and treat them with more generosity and helpfulness, even if they got in trouble.

Another study was a little bit sly. Interviewers asked random people on a college campus if they'd be willing to speak for a few minutes about the most positive thing that had happened to them in the previous five years in exchange for one dollar. After hearing the experience and asking questions of the respondent, each interviewer reacted in preplanned, various ways: positively, neutrally, or negatively.

After each conversation completed, the interviewer handed the respondent their payment in a sealed envelope and walked away. But each envelope contained *two* dollars. The extra dollar was snuck in as a "mistake" to see whether the subjects would flag the questioners down and give it back.

You probably won't be surprised to learn that the ones who received positive affirmations were more likely to return the extra dollar—68% of them, in fact, did just that. On the other hand, only 36% of the subjects that got critical or disinterested responses returned the overpayment. The findings imply that validation encourages other qualities of generosity and honesty and that *invalidating* someone inhibits their using those attributes.

In a third study, a selection of participants was instructed to concentrate on the best experience they'd had in the previous three years. Then they were matched with another person and encouraged to tell them about that experience. Unbeknownst to them, that other person was not a subject in the study but someone (a "confederate" as the researchers put it) who'd been trained to respond in a favorable way to their experience.

Other participants in the study were matched with confederates under the pretense that they too were just participants in the study. Instead of talking about their positive experience, though, they participated in a "fun" activity that involved drawing.

The feedback from the respondents after the third experiment showed an interesting split. Subjects who took part in the fun activity reported liking their partners more and that they'd enjoyed their time with them more than those who'd only spoken with them. But those who had discussed their experience and gotten a supportive response reported that they *trusted* the other person more and that they were more likely to be open with their private thoughts and feelings with those confederates.

All three studies showed the secret power of validation in our everyday lives. These affirmations caused test subjects to feel even better about their positive experiences. They felt more assured about the daily, basic structures of their lives and generated a large amount of goodwill in return. They got another level of satisfaction and value on top of the original experience—all from a somewhat simple act of validation.

It's important to note that the positive events the subjects were talking about were not all major milestones that are commonly validated on a mass level—positive life-changers like graduation, marriage, or childbirth. Most of them were simply happy experiences or interactions, things that happen more commonly. But the validation of these smaller events was just as significant to the subjects, if not more. Getting supportive remarks about them fostered conditions of trust and confidence, not to mention generosity in return.

Furthermore, the positive outcome doubles back and rewards the validator. The goodwill flows both ways in the interaction. There's the initial satisfaction of having generated positivity in someone else, which is almost always the preferable outcome in an interaction. The long-lasting effects are significant as well: by benefitting someone else's support system, we create an arena of kindness for the relationship. When *we* need validation, confidence, or support from that relationship in the future, the strength of the relationship will make it easier to meet those needs.

Validation Basics

Any verbal interaction looks simple on paper, but sometimes we can get tripped up on execution. Validation is no different: There are steps one must deliberately take to make it work. When someone confides in us or expresses a certain immediate emotion, they're looking to have that emotion processed and accepted by whomever they're talking with. That validation doesn't always happen. Validation is intentional in generating an outcome of goodwill and importance, so there are certainly ways to go about it correctly and incorrectly.

There are two main components of an act of validation that define its success.

Identifying the emotion. While recognizing our own emotions is a crucial part of our personal mental health, being able to do so with someone else is a big plus in our relationship and social health. Being able to verbalize our interpretation of our partner's emotions—*before* they have to come right out and say "I'm angry" or "I'm sad"—opens the door to a positive validation. It shows that we're keyed in on what they're communicating, that we're really listening and not just hearing.

Justifying the emotion. Once we've identified what our communication partner is feeling, the next step is proclaiming it as a proper— or at least very understandable—emotional reaction: "Why, if *I* was in your shoes, I'd feel the same way too!" This establishes a sense of commonality, that our partner's sentiments are exactly what rational people would feel under the circumstances. It communicates that you are feeling the same emotion they are and emphasizes that the way they feel and think is justified.

Justifying your partner's feelings is a much more important component than instantly offering advice on what to do. They want to feel that you empathize with their plight first, before hearing what corrective measures they should take. Even well-intentioned or accurate advice would simply infer that they've been doing something wrong or that their emotional status is primarily their fault. Before giving advice, we need to connect with them on a sympathetic, emotional level. That will make working through a solution much easier and more supportive later. Oftentimes the act of validation, not advice, is really what people are seeking in an interaction. This tells us emotional support is more important than having a to-do list to fix someone's circumstances or feelings; indeed, feeling better about something is *far more* important than knowing what to do about it.

How do these two parts work in real communication? Let's first imagine a scenario that *doesn't* work:

> *Partner 1:* "I can't believe this! I'm getting heat at work for something my boss told me to do! I knew it was a bad idea, I protested it, they forced me to do it, it messed things up royally, and now my boss told me I'd have to work overtime this weekend to put everything back the way it was!"
>
> *Partner 2:* "I told you that place was a disaster before you took the job. You

shouldn't be surprised this is happening."

Partner 1: "Gee, thanks for making me feel worse."

Partner 2: "I'm not the one who wanted to go into the funeral home business. Don't look at me. Why don't you look for another job?"

What's wrong with Partner 2's response? Just about everything. Partner 1 was upset at what they perceived as an unfair situation. They felt upset that they weren't taken seriously at work and then got shafted when things went wrong. Partner 2 is essentially doing the exact same thing. By reminding Partner 1 that "I told you so," Partner 2 isn't taking their feelings seriously either. They set up the judgment that they made the wrong choice to begin with and shouldn't feel upset because, essentially, they made their bed and have to lie in it.

This exchange is much more on the mark:

Partner 1: "I can't believe this! I'm getting heat at work for something my boss told me to do! I knew it was a bad idea, I protested it, they forced me to do it, it messed things up royally, and now my boss told me I'd have to work overtime this weekend to put everything back the way it was!"

Partner 2: "Did they really do that? No! That's infuriating! I'd be livid about it too."

Partner 1: "I just feel like I don't have any control over my own destiny at that place."

Partner 2: "That must be really disheartening. I don't see how anyone would feel otherwise under such conditions, especially at a funeral home."

In that exchange, Partner 2 is much better. They've identified the emotion Partner 1 is feeling, namely fury ("That's infuriating!"). They then established the emotion as proper or understandable and exactly the way people would feel in that situation ("I'd be livid about it myself"). Partner 2 then repeats the process in the last statement: Partner 1 feels "disheartened," and anyone in those circumstances would feel and act the same.

Note that in the second exchange Partner 2 does not try to fix the problem or even necessarily make deliberate steps to make Partner 1 feel *that* much better. Partner 1 needs to feel enraged at the moment; it's a justifiable emotion. If Partner 2 had tried to force a solution by giving advice or suggesting something else, it would have interrupted Partner 1's emotional process. It would have been an effort to stop Partner 1 from feeling how they're entirely entitled to feel.

What's more important is that Partner 1 feel validated in their response, that they're understood and empathized with. That reinforces the quality of their communication. If there happens to be a way Partner 2 can effectively offer help or work through a solution later, great. But without a sense that the partner's feelings are valid, that effort won't amount to much. Even if you know what must be done and think someone is idiotic for engaging in self-defeating behaviors, think of it this way: they can't understand it unless they hear themselves say it. So you must humor them and engage in a certain degree of their drama to successfully validate and get them to their end goals of emotional support and perhaps even a solution.

Validating and invalidating responses. In the first example above, Partner 2's responses are inappropriate because they derail Partner 1's legitimate emotions. Partner 2 doesn't want to spend time focusing on Partner 1 for whatever reason—they just don't want to deal with them. So Partner 2's ill-mannered, terse, and mean reaction make a bad situation worse.

But not all such responses are meant in a bad way—one can also, unsuspectingly, invalidate someone's feelings with good intentions. Some of the more innocuous responses we give to someone's emotional tumult can actually hurt them without us realizing what's going on. This is most likely what most of us are doing when we *think* we're validating; in fact, we're making the situation worse.

For example, when consoling someone over a situation that makes them nervous or apprehensive, one might say something like *"Don't worry about it"* or *"You shouldn't feel that way."* And they might say it in a comforting tone to make them feel better. They mean well.

But such responses are actually invalidating. They *are* worried about their situation; they *already* feel that way. Telling someone they're not acting in the optimal way negates their entitlement to their own feelings. Even if you're making that remark out of kindness, your partner may receive it as invalidation of their perfectly normal feelings. It's simply unhelpful to hear, similar to telling someone, *"Hey, just grow taller."*

An alternative response that successfully validates the other partner might be *"I can sense that you're worried about this situation."* This response assures the partner that their concerns are real and that their presence is rightful. Remember, your goal is to identify emotions and then justify them—nothing more.

Another invalidating and unhelpful response is *"I'm sorry you feel that way."* You might think the phrase "I'm sorry" is a form of empathy. And in a way it can be. But it can also be interpreted as an empty sentiment. If someone's lost their job, been evicted, come down with a debilitating disease, or suffered some other awful injury or fate, "I'm sorry" doesn't quite cut it. By saying you're sorry someone is undergoing emotional turmoil—that they "feel that way"—you're also suggesting that there's a way they *should* feel but they're not. Whether they *should* feel a certain way is irrelevant because they *do* feel that way.

A more validating option would be *"I can understand why you're feeling this way—I think anyone else would too."* Explaining that they have a right to be uneasy and that such feelings are normal help relax their tension and produce a bond with the rest of the world: they wouldn't be alone in feeling this way. Even if you think you *wouldn't* feel the exact way they feel, it's important to establish that others *would*. (Besides, you might not really know if you wouldn't feel that way anyway—it probably hasn't happened to you yet.)

Likewise, responses like *"At least it's not like…"* or *"It could be worse"* imply that your partner's concerns are illogical or unfounded. Emotions are never logical, but they *are* real. Maybe the issue *can* be worse, but not right in someone's subjective sense of reality. Objective comparisons to more dire situations serve to put the worrier "in their place," even if they're meant to make the partner feel less bad in the short term. But they're just friendlier marginalization. The judgment as to whether someone's situation can or can't be worse belongs to the person who's feeling the emotions.

In this situation, a proper validating response would make the listener feel that they're being taken seriously: *"You've really been through a lot"* or *"Tell me more about what you're feeling."* These responses acknowledge the weight of the other person's issues, reassuring them that you're willing to take their worries seriously and don't want to minimize how bad they feel.

Outright rejections are not just invalidations but straight-up reproaches: *"I'm not having this discussion!"* This is invalidating because it directly cuts off communication and even further says that the other person's concerns are unworthy. By saying this, the respondent imposes a limit on communications—obviously there are some subjects that they're unwilling to discuss with you, when a true friend or partner wouldn't have any hands-off topics whatsoever.

A better response is *"Would you like some help working through this problem?"* or (again) *"Tell me more about what you're feeling."* This helps the partner feel like they have, if not a total solution, then at least an open path to finding a better result.

If it sounds like I'm suggesting you walk on eggshells when dealing with other people's feelings and one of these responses slips out—don't. You will make one of those responses again when you're done with this book. So will I, to be honest, because you and I both mean well. But be aware that those responses are invalidations that should be followed up as quickly as possible with validating statements. Remember that you're trying to form a connection and make communication flow freely. That will make the pivot easier to make.

Gottman's Emotional Bids

Researcher John Gottman of the University of Washington was interested in finding out why some relationships thrived and others faltered. He also wondered whether there were cues in couples' routine interactions that could work as general predictors as to a given couple's likelihood of maintaining a successful partnership.

To find out, Gottman outfitted his laboratory to resemble a bed and breakfast inn, and he invited 130 newlywed couples to spend a day in the environment. He encouraged the couples to just go about the day as they normally would: fixing meals, having conversations, relaxing as if they were at home. The room was equipped with cameras, sensors, computers, and other data collection devices. News media called

Gottman's research room "The Love Lab." After the couples' stay, Gottman followed up on their lives for six years.

Throughout the couples' time in the lab, Gottman picked up on extremely subtle communication patterns. To the naked eye and ear, many of these exchanges were almost unnoticeable—in fact, they were largely mundane and ordinary: "Check out that car across the street." "That's an interesting tablecloth pattern." "I think cilantro gives this dish a little kick." In other words, they were extremely boring.

But what the conversations were about wasn't important. Rather, Gottman interpreted even the smallest of communication techniques as requests for some kind of *connection*. Speakers were asking their partners to exhibit an interest or recognition that they could share with them. These asks took both verbal and nonverbal forms: in addition to direct questions, they included gestures, facial expressions, certain physical movements, and contact. Gottman called these seemingly trivial cues "bids." Of course, these are calls for validation by another name. As Gottman discovered, bids were not always validated.

Responses to these bids were classified into two categories. A positive or affirming reply was "turning toward"—the partner gave the bidder a response that connected the two. Negative, neutral, or apathetic responses were labeled "turning away."

For example, let's consider the riveting exchange about the tablecloth pattern. A "turning toward" response might consist of a raised eyebrow and a remark like "Yeah, that *is* an interesting tablecloth pattern. Look at all the interesting angles." It could even just be the raised eyebrow and a nod with no words. A "turning away" response, on the other hand, might consist of a furrowed brow and a declaration like "We're here in this nicely furnished Love Lab and you're talking about a stupid tablecloth pattern?" A neutral response, like a silent shoulder shrug, would also fall under the "turning away" category.

The content of a "turning toward" message goes much deeper than the words or expressions used. Even the most trivial "turning toward" response shows a bedrock of concern and interest in the partner. You're not merely saying, "This may be the greatest tablecloth pattern ever produced." You're actually saying, "I'm listening to you. I'm paying attention to you. I'm interested in you. Your feelings and opinions are important to me." In other words, you're validating.

Gottman theorized that these extremely minor interactions might hold a clue as to the soundness of the couples' relationships. Those couples who showed a tendency to validate each other's bids—whether they knew it or not—would be more caring and supportive of each other in regular practice. Those who dismissed or criticized the bids would have a lot less to sustain them.

The results were pretty clear-cut. In his reviews of the couples six years after their visits, Gottman found that couples who remained together responded to bids with "turn toward" messages 87% of their time in the lab and had their emotional needs met nine times out of ten. Couples who divorced had "turn toward" rates of only 33%.

But here's the stunning part. Through his method, Gottman was able to predict each couple's future based on the data from his experiments. He forecasted whether couples would stay together and be happy, stay together and be *un*happy, or break up. Gottman's predictions of who would get divorced had a whopping accuracy rate of *93.6%*. That's beyond startling and proves almost without exception that validation is an essential part of deep relationships.

The implications of Gottman's findings go far beyond the married couples he studied—they hold true in other interpersonal relationships we have: friends, coworkers, and siblings. Kids who turn toward their classmates or playmates generally make friends more readily. Sisters and brothers who are accepting and supportive of each other are more likely to retain that closeness throughout their lives.

Turning away, on the other hand, shuts down that access and serves as rejection. Kids who bully other kids cut themselves off from forming good relationships (in fact, they may be doing so because their own bids to their parents may have gone rejected). Couples who fight a lot, or aggressively change the subject when the other is talking, harm themselves bit by bit.

Even if the rejected bidder doesn't act or seem to get hurt when their bid is turned away, they don't forget it. And they let their sour emotions build up. At some point, this buildup reaches critical mass and the bidder starts showing visible frustration. Soon they start verbalizing their anger toward people who reject them, which brings about a combative pattern that gets instilled in the relationship. There is usually no reversing that pattern: the relationship does not survive this lack of validation.

What if we want to provide "turning toward" bids but don't always pick up when our friends and loved ones are making them? Bids are usually not obvious; they're usually very discreet and unclear and probably not consciously made by the bidder.

That's because the bid is an emotional display that we need validation. It comes from a defenseless position: we need connection and confirmation of our feelings, and that need makes us less secure and more vulnerable. So it's not possible to be totally direct with a bid because we're trying to guard our emotions at the same time.

So does the respondent have to be hyper-aware and overly dramatic every time someone makes a bid? *"That's the greatest idea I've ever heard! You're so correct it's astounding! You are a god walking this earth!"*

Of course not. That's not practical, and it's not realistic. No relationship has a bid acceptance rate of 100%. Everyone messes up from time to time. Researchers found that husbands in solid marriages *still* neglected their wives' bids 19% of the time. Husbands in marriages doomed for divorce showed a tendency that was nearly the mathematical opposite: they only accepted their wives' bids 18% of the time.

While you'll never be perfect, you *can* get better at giving and recognizing bids. It's just a matter of being more attentive to the frequent small exchanges that make up those bids and their responses. When your partner or friend texts you to see how you're doing, instead of treating it like one of the thousands of messages you get, give it a prompt and affectionate response. Remember, they're just seeking a connection and minor validation from you.

If you want to take this practice even further, you can devise what author Eric Barker calls a "bid roadmap" for the people closest to you. This is simply keeping a written catalog of what your bidding relationship is like with them. How do your bids (and theirs) usually come out? Which responses work and which ones don't? What happens when you get a "turn-away" bid, and what do you think is behind it? (If it sounds a little, let's say, *creepy* to keep a catalog, just consider it a highly organized diary. That's basically all it is. You're recording what you perceive about the people closest to you and giving it some context.)

Relationship skills, like validation, are just like every other skill in the universe: they take practice. We tend to think our interpersonal connections are predestined and automatic, based on how strong or weak our "chemistry" with those people may be. But that's not the case. Even the most compatible partners need to learn and relearn how to communicate effectively and with consideration. Similarly, being a solid listener and communicator can produce friendships or relationships with others that didn't seem possible at first meeting.

By building on those skills you can read people's signals without presumption, which is important. Negative expressions like sorrow, rage, or dread are all linked to a need that's not being met. If you can identify that need, or even come reasonably *close*, you're opening yourself up to more meaningful exchanges and relationships.

Six Steps of Validation

As helpful as it is to understand the nuances of Gottman's bids, some may find them a little too indirect in helping them understand how to validate, especially if they're just starting to learn. That's okay. Practicing relationship skills also means being fair to yourself about where you are in the process.

In that case, learning the six steps of validation as outlined by Kate Thieda might be a better place to start. Making up a sort of checklist of conscious reactions, these steps are a lot more precise for those who want to start at the beginning. And they're easy to follow. When your friend or loved one is in a vulnerable state and is reaching out, these are the stages and the order you should go through to effectively hear and communicate with them.

1. Be present. First of all, show up. This is at once the easiest and trickiest step of all. It doesn't mean just being physically present and maintaining eye contact. Being present is actually more like two smaller steps: giving your partner your absolute attention, then being accommodating and understanding that they're having big emotions at the moment.

The first part is physical: it just means eliminating distractions. Turn off your phone, switch off the TV, and reduce the volume of music to a hum in the background. (You could also just turn it off, but relaxing music can make the environment for communication a little easier.) It's obviously more complicated in a public place—if it's easy to move to a quieter spot, do so. If not, try to ward off distractions by keeping complete visual focus on your partner and leaning in to hear if you have to.

The second part means accepting your partner's strong feelings—showing up in a sensitive way. We can react too quickly to a display of intense emotion, and it's fair to feel initially startled when someone's severely sad or angry. As soon as the shock recedes, though, it's crucial to let your partner know you want to deal with them as they are. You can do this by asking an open-ended question: *"Tell me what's going on," "What are you feeling right now?"* or *"Can you talk about what happened?"* You should also watch and soften your visual and facial cues to let your partner know you're open to hearing and not ready to judge.

2. Accurate reflection. After you've listened to your partner explain what's happening, the next step is to show that you're concentrating on their well-being and trying to understand what they're feeling. That's when you try to offer an accurate reflection of what they've just expressed. Reflection can take different forms, but they are all verbal statements that mirror the emotions your partner is conveying, provide context, and assure them that their feelings are comprehended. *"I sense that you're disappointed about not getting that job"* or *"I can hear your anxiety about having to deal with your family at Thanksgiving."*

It doesn't have to be more than a sentence or two of acknowledgment—in fact, it shouldn't be. It should be just enough to let your partner know that you're hearing them, that you've invested your interest and concern and want to hear them continue their story.

Also try to paraphrase their feelings in your own words instead of just repeating what they've said to you word for word. Simply echoing their statements verbatim only proves that you have a good short-term memory. Rephrasing it in your own language, though, shows that you're trying to *understand* them on a deeper level. (Plus, parroting something back to someone could be mistaken for sarcasm, like an adult mimicking a crying child.)

3. Reading behavior and guessing what they're feeling. For a variety of reasons, many of us are detached from and out of touch with our emotions. A big cause of this separation is having experienced invalidation in the past. Our parents may have neglected our feelings as kids (like that mimicking parent does in the last paragraph, for example). Or perhaps we've tried to be honest about our feelings with others before and their reactions were so harmful that now we repress our emotions and keep them buried.

That's why the next step is guessing how your partner feels by how they're behaving: *"I'm guessing you're feeling rejected by your parents because they're not showing confidence in your decisions"* or *"It sounds to me like you're frustrated with your coworker because they're not keeping their commitments."*

It's vital to frame this statement as a *guess*, not a firm declaration of your belief or diagnosis of the situation. Being assertive sets you in a position where you're superior to them and you know the answers to their problems. That creates a distance, a sort of mentor-student relationship that might make them less forthcoming, not to mention resentful. This is a step beyond reflecting emotions, because you aren't waiting for them to express themselves. You are taking the lead here and trying to lead them to an emotional resolution.

Another reason you need to present your interpretation of their feelings as a guess is, of course, that you might be wrong. In this step, being wrong is completely okay. You're trying to figure out what their emotions are. But ultimately, they're the ones who are feeling their emotions, and they know best what those are. If you guessed wrong, they might correct you. That, too, is completely okay. Give them a safe environment to explain themselves. If they know you're just guessing, they'll feel more secure in clarifying what's happening with them.

4. Understand their behavior in the context of their lives. This step depends on your having knowledge of your partner's past history and general makeup—and if you've been close for a long time, you should know that history reasonably well. All the reactions we have now are the product of events and experiences that we had in the past, as well as the way we're biologically constructed. In this validation step, you express a connection with their behavior by understanding how the past has shaped their actions and feelings.

For example, let's say your friend was hit by a car while he or she was riding their bike as a child. The injuries weren't serious but the event was understandably traumatic. Particularly since it happened when they were very young and impressionable, they may feel fearful about getting on a bike or crossing the street in heavy traffic.

That's a somewhat simple example in which everyone turned out relatively okay in the end (though it sucked at the time). But be aware there are many more serious and painful experiences for your partner that may be at play. They may have endured abuse, suffered from the early death of their parents, seen terrible violence in wartime or combat, or some other intense tragedy. You should tread with a little care in these instances—and your response should reflect that care. *"Knowing how you lost your mother at an early age, I think I understand why you're afraid of abandonment." "I imagine you can't easily trust someone after being in that abusive relationship."*

5. Normalize or affirm their emotional reactions. When something happens that causes a big reaction in us, it's a unique and new event—it's not a normal occurrence. It causes us to feel something we don't feel in the usual course of our lives. But it's important to validate that. Although the situation isn't normal, our partner's emotional reactions to that unusual situation are entirely normal.

For example, getting fired from a job isn't a small deal. It's a rare happening that can cause a lot of extreme stress and trauma. Someone who just got fired may be feeling anxious and worried for their future—and it's very important for them to know that anxiety and worry are completely proper things to feel. *"If I just got laid off, I'd feel nervous about the future too."* Your partner must understand that their reactions are not bizarre or wrong; they need to feel that others would feel the same way if they were going through it.

However, when affirming their feelings as normal, it's important to *not* say something like *"You'll be fine"* or *"It's gonna be okay."* Those statements, well-intended as they are, actually invalidate your partner's feelings by effectively ending the discussion, negating the effect of their hard feelings. You actually *don't* know if it's going to be fine. Even if your historical experiences with those feelings have turned out to be okay, that doesn't mean *theirs* will.

A preferable option would be *"I have faith in your ability to get through this"*—but even that's not completely necessary at this point. Your partner's feelings should be center stage. And they have to know that they are. Your being able to comprehend and validate how they feel is much more important to them right now. They need to be able to complete that expression on their own, without getting cut off by a nice sentiment that means well.

6. Radical genuineness. This is related to the previous stage of normalizing your partner's feelings and goes a step further. At the end of your communication, your partner should feel that they're real people experiencing valid feelings and *not* like someone who's crazy and incompetent. Your endgame should result in your partner feeling loved and taken seriously—that you consider them your equal and that they're just going through an exceptionally hard time at the moment.

This might be a good time for the expression *"I have faith you'll get through this,"* since it relates to their being a normal person in a challenging situation. But it's important to establish that *you* believe

them to be that way— that you know
they're able to solve their problems or
adapt to changes, that they're not helpless
or unable to make anything right. This is the
definition of radical genuineness: treating
and supporting your loved one as a human
being that you trust and believe in,
especially when they're down.

Quick Ways to Respect and Validate at Your Best

Making a sustained commitment to showing
honor and validating your partner is a
worthy policy that's worth the time and
practice. But there are other, smaller ways
that a strong friend or mate can show
respect and keep communications strong.

*Show your awareness of your partner's needs
and desires by acting on your discoveries or
knowledge about them.* A husband and wife
went on a three-week vacation to a distant
place. The day they returned home was long
and exhausting, and they weren't looking
forward to having to make dinner when
they finally got home. But when they did,
they discovered the wife's friend had left a
care package of food on their doorstep. The

friend knew the couple's itinerary and they weren't going to be in a mood to make dinner themselves.

This kind of deed is one of the most powerful ways to show your awareness and concern for a friend or loved one's needs: doing something preemptively based on what you know about them. These kinds of small surprise gifts make a very lasting impression on whoever receives them. Giving them is a solid way to express your validation of their thoughts and desires without them mentioning it.

Act on your partner's requests in a timely manner. When you partner expresses something they need from you, don't delay your response unnecessarily. If they need you to run an errand, ask you for help in completing a project, or request your opinion on anything from home furnishings to politics, be timely and considerate in your response. Don't be hesitant or stall your response—being prompt shows the depth of your consideration.

Be aware of the ways you might show contempt—and get rid of them. Contempt is an expression of disfavor that implies our partner's feelings and statements are not worthy and deserve to be ridiculed or mocked. There are several ways to reveal contempt. Whether it's a verbal quality like being sharp or impatient or a nonverbal cue like rolling your eyes and shaking your head, the slightest and shortest expression can cause more hurt than you might think. When you're dealing with your communication partner about things they're truly concerned about, be cognizant of those invalidating responses and prevent yourself from making them.

Be understanding when your partner makes mistakes or poor choices. Centuries of scientific research have proven that 100% of all humans make mistakes. Sometimes these mistakes are unforced, and sometimes they're deliberate choices. Try to be compassionate and understanding when your partner or friend makes a mistake at work or adopts a lifestyle choice that doesn't seem to be a good decision. Encourage them that every mistake we make, even prolonged ones, is something we can learn from.

Show appreciation and admiration for your partner's gifts. Maybe your friend's a trivia master. They could be a great baker. They may have an extraordinary way with words. They may have a talent for analysis, athletics, music, or juggling. Everyone has special gifts, and everyone wants attention and appreciation for them even if they don't say it. Find active ways to compliment and support your loved ones for their unique abilities—or even their common abilities that they do rather well.

Accommodate your partner's style and ways of getting things done. Some people like to blow through action items in a certain task. If they're cleaning their kitchen, they won't stop until every surface is spotless and all items are in their right places. Other people are more deliberate. Maybe they like to plan how they're going to clean the kitchen before they actually do it. The point is, everyone has a different approach to common problems or tasks, and none of them are wrong. Be accepting of the different methods and ways your loved ones go about their lives and business and make room for their unique approaches.

There's more than one way to get most jobs done.

Relationships emerge from feelings of love, happiness, and satisfaction. But they're *preserved* by shaping those sentiments into practicing validation and respect, and that takes work and conscientiousness. When those positive reinforcements happen and our partners feel accepted and esteemed, it helps communication take place and always improve.

Takeaways:

- Validation is the act of showing respect and acknowledgment to people's intentions and emotions. It can be as easy as nodding your head, but it can also go much deeper for greater impact and respect.

- At the most basic level, it consists of identifying people's emotions and then justifying them. You first act as a detective to understand what you are dealing with and then make people feel that they are completely rational in feeling their emotions. Emotions are never quite rational, but they are always real.

- Many times when we try to validate, we are actually worsening the situation by using invalidating statements. These are statements that dismiss or minimize people's feelings, such as "Oh, you'll be fine" or "You shouldn't feel that way!" They feel more prescriptive and try to convince people to see the bright side of things—but that's not what they are interested in at the moment.

- A helpful six-step path to validation is as follows: being present, accurately reflecting emotions, guessing emotions, understanding emotions in context, affirming emotions, and then being honest.

- Validation is one of the ultimate shows of respect. But there are other ways to subtly show respect and caring for others. They center around awareness, action, appreciation, and, most importantly, attention.

Chapter 5. Shut Up and Listen

Raise your hand if this has ever happened to you: you are speaking with someone, and immediately after you finished speaking, they ignored absolutely everything you said, didn't even acknowledge it, and continued on their separate thought or tangent? It's as if they didn't hear a word of what you said, and they probably didn't.

Can you imagine this happening during a theater performance?

Actor #1: "I want to go to the butcher shop now, so let's go!"
Actor #2: "This table is fascinating. Do you

think it was made in Germany?"
Actor #1: "Uh... so back to that butcher shop..."

Actor #1 would be left confused and scrambling. Unfortunately, if we're honest with ourselves, this type of interaction is common and happens often. For all of our good intentions, most people are terrible listeners, us included, and it impacts the quality of our relationships. People want to say what they want to say, and they are more interested in their own lives than anyone else's. To most, on an unconscious level, *sharing* is caring, not listening.

This is normal human nature, but that doesn't mean we should kowtow to it. This book is about better communication, which occasionally goes against our instincts, so we need to stop the habit of not listening and simply shut up more.

Solid communication is a two-way street, and you have to give the other person space to speak in order to receive it for yourself. Unfortunately, for many people (hopefully not you), conversation is seen as a dumping ground. This will happen in one of two ways.

People will either come in with a fixed agenda and set of talking points or they will be so wrapped up in their own lives that they just want to share it with you and not hear about yours. In either case, they open their mouths, unload information, and don't stop until they get tired of their own voices.

How does this make the listener feel? People aren't dumb. People can detect when you are engaged and interested in what they have to say.

They will get the distinct feeling that the other person is just waiting for their turn to speak and are not interested in anything they have to say. It's like they know they are doing their best to try to listen to you, but they feel that their lives are so much more captivating that they can't resist going back to that topic.

The listeners are not getting much out of the exchange, and at some point, only listening to someone and having your prompts ignored is burdensome and flat-out annoying. In a theater performance, the two parties won't be working together, and the scene will be disjointed as one person will have to keep catering to the other person's whims.

Silence is an effective communication tool. Use it more frequently than you think you should. If anyone you engage with answers your questions happily but doesn't pause to ask you how you're doing, then *they* need to shut up more. If that's you, *you're* the one who needs to shut up more.

It can be difficult because sometimes we build up a lot of steam during conversations. We feel like we're on a roll with what we're talking about, and we could talk about it for hours. That's a selfish pursuit, and if someone wants to hog the spotlight for a while, you must absolutely surrender the spotlight and be willing to derail yourself and jump completely into someone else's ideas and topics.

Therefore, in conversation, one of the first keys is that you don't just wait for your turn to speak. To some, this sounds like "let people speak and don't interrupt them," but it goes deeper than that.

This actually means to empty your mind and stop composing your response or the next topic while someone is speaking. When you are listening, you aren't only waiting for your turn to speak and preparing for that. You are listening with a blank slate and then tailoring your response directly to what was just said. Wherever the other person wants to derail the conversation to, you must be willing to go with them. That's great listening and a showing of respect.

If you are letting the other person speak simply because you feel like you shouldn't be speaking for so long at one stretch, you are just waiting for your turn to speak. You aren't participating in the conversation; you are giving a monologue in the hopes that the other person contributes and listens to it. Or worse yet, the other person listens in a similar fashion to you and you are in a case of dueling monologues versus a dialogue.

Worse yet, you are not respecting them. It tells them you do not value them enough to listen while you are waiting for your turn to unload what you have to say. Much of this is subconscious, so it would be wrong to say that we are malicious in our daily conversations. We sometimes get too eager to talk about ourselves because our lives are most interesting to us, so why wouldn't they be to others?

We're like puppies discovering snow for the first time and are unable to contain our excitement.

We already had an example of poor listening earlier—that damned butcher shop. However, it was egregious, and most examples of poor listening are subtler and you may not even realize that they are bad. They might merely be classified as "ineffective."

Ineffective listening:

Bob: I heard that butcher shop is pretty good.
Johnson: Oh, cool. Where is it?

Bob: About a ten-minute walk.

Johnson: Oh, I see. Did I tell you about my new niece?

Bob: No, you didn't. Congratulations.

Johnson: She's really cute. Here are some pictures.

The reason this is ineffective listening is because Johnson merely pays lip service to Bob's interests before being unable to contain himself from talking about his niece. He doesn't see Bob's thought to completion and cuts him off in the middle to shift to his own topic. This is the type of poor listening that we encounter more on a daily basis. It's subtle but just as bad sometimes.

Here is that conversation but with better listening:

Bob: I heard that butcher shop is pretty good.

Johnson: Oh, cool. Where is it?

Bob: About a ten-minute walk.

Johnson: Oh, I see. Did you want to check it out?

Bob: I do. Do you want to come with me?

Johnson: Sure. Along the way, I can show you pictures of my new niece.

Both parties are able to wedge their thoughts in. Conversation that improves relationships and makes people feel positive about each other involves an interplay between silence and speaking, and both parties have an equal opportunity to take the spotlight.

Collaboration is the name of the game, and waiting for your turn to speak doesn't contribute to a shared goal—only yours.

Interrupting, of course, is also a no-no in the quest for better listening. Interrupting sends the message of "I know you were talking, but what I have to say is more interesting for both of us" or "What I'm saying is more important than what you say." Again, it's not conscious, but that's what happens when we put our thoughts and agendas over those of other people.

You might think it's a big deal, but if you keep interrupting, that is precisely the message you send. Your conversation partner doesn't know what's going on inside your head, so who can blame them for feeling alienated if your actions don't represent your intentions?

Here are a few quick guidelines for interruptions. First, don't interrupt others unless you agree with them so emphatically that you can finish their sentence with them. Second, if you do interrupt them for any reason, ask them immediately after you finish speaking what they were saying and bring it back to them. Acknowledge your error and quickly put the spotlight back onto them.

Third, try to abide by the two-second rule to police yourself. After someone finishes speaking, pause for a full two seconds while contemplating what they've said and externally demonstrate that you are analyzing their words. Then, and only then, may you reply. This will get you into the habit of thinking before speaking and addressing people first.

You can also get into the habit of using phrases that encourage them to keep speaking. It's not always enough to just shut up and nod your head. Staring blankly at someone will make people feel like they have to repeat themselves and that their message didn't get through. It has the same exact effect as not listening to them.

You have to demonstrate that you are mentally following every step of the conversation, even if you aren't. Use your facial expressions, eyebrows, gestures, and laughs to signal a reaction to each of their statements. Nod when they emphasize a point. We'll cover this in greater detail shortly when we address active listening, but here are some encouraging phrases such as the following to show interest and investment:

- Uh huh.
- I see.
- That's interesting.
- Tell me more.
- And then?
- What happened next?
- What about that?

If you look at conversations as simply an exercise to be heard and shine a spotlight on your ego, you are doing a great disservice to everyone you engage with. Not everyone is as interested in your life as you are. Even if you think you are listening and shutting up sufficiently, there's a chance that you still cling to your train of thought subconsciously and are waiting for the opportunity to assert them.

To improve your conversations and connect better, you need to shut up more. As the old saying goes, you can't learn when you're speaking.

Listening is actually one of the most self-interested things you can do, because you are the person who benefits and learns. It's a complete win-win situation.

To see the simple power of shutting up more, make your next conversation with a friend all about them. Try to find out about every minute detail of their day. This means you shutting up, listening to them, reacting accordingly, and asking questions that go deeper. Say as little as you can while reacting properly and moving the conversation along in whatever direction they want. Make it as unbalanced a conversation as possible.

Don't interrupt them, and try to coax as many stories from them as possible. Note how willing they are to speak about themselves in detail.

Is this easy or difficult for you? Did it feel unnatural to ask people deeply about their day and focus on them? If it did, then you just might need to practice shutting up more!

By the way, much of what has been discussed regarding listening thus far is about how to resist your selfish tendencies to seize the spotlight and share to your heart's content. But if you have that, so does the person across from you. Step aside and give *them* the chance to be selfish in an effort to better your communication.

Five Levels of Listening

Just as communication has its given levels from idle small talk to soul-baring confession and revelation, so does the art of listening. It's not as simple as simply flipping a switch to change from inattention to total concentration. Solid communication takes working through each of these levels, often in a conscious way.

There are five different levels of listening that we experience, from total ignorance to almost consuming attention. Most of our lives we sort of float through the first four levels, which all reflect at least a measure of self-interest. In other words, in those four levels we still use our own references in those stages to interpret what the other person is saying (if we're listening at all). Many of us can hope to get to level 4 at best, and even that stage we can turn out to be a bit deceptive.

In all truth, some of us never quite get to the deepest level 5, even though it's the most important level and the one we should shoot for. It involves total focus and absorption in what our partner is saying. Getting there is exceptionally rare and hard to maintain. But in order to drive communication in a relationship forward, it's vital that we try to get to that deepest level.

Here, then, are the levels we're talking about:

1. Ignoring

2. Pretend listening

3. Selective listening

4. Attentive listening

5. Empathetic listening

1. Ignoring

I'm betting this level is obvious: it's not listening at all—an ostrich with its head in the sand. Whether you're distracted, consumed with something else, or flat-out don't care, ignorance is an immediate discouragement to anyone who's trying to speak to you.

> *Person A:* I'm worried about our son. He's spending an awful lot of time

online and doesn't interact with anyone in the real world anymore.

Person B:

Person A: It's like he's got no interest in forming real relationships with anybody. It's got me quite concerned.

Person B:

Person A: Hello?

Person B:

Person A: Also, he just drove our minivan into the river and is sacrificing animals to the Dark Lord in our living room.

Person B:

Person A: Are you hearing a word I'm saying?

Person B: Hey, look at that squirrel!

There's not much to be said about this level. It's bad communication at its worst. Person B is utterly uninterested in Person A's point of view and makes no effort to say anything until something catches their personal interest. This first level of communication is important to get out of ASAP. (But keep in mind, someone not being *able* to hear you is not ignorance, so speak up if you can.)

2. Pretend Listening

This happens most prevalently in face-to-face communication. We *look* like we're paying attention, but we're not entirely engaged with what our partner is saying. Our eyes might get that distant look, and we just don't appear to be "all there." We make the slightest cues imaginable just to appear that we're taking in everything. But in reality, we're kind of phoning it in, like a bored hall monitor.

> *Person A:* I had a talk with my sister the other day. Her husband's been staying long hours at the office. I think she suspects something.
>
> *Person B:* Mm-hmm.
>
> *Person A:* I mean, I know she can get a little overly dramatic and unduly suspicious. But he can't have that

much work to do. Not so much that he misses four dinners a week.

Person B: Yes.

Person A: I kind of think she might have cause for concern. Don't you?

Person B: Yeah. Wait, what?

Person A: Have you really heard anything I'm saying?

Person B: Uh... hey, look. That squirrel's back again.

The level 2 listener is making only a superficial effort to convince their partner that they're involved in the conversation so as not to appear rude. But of course, they're still preoccupied with their own thoughts and concerns. They stay at the baseline minimum, and it can be frustrating to anyone trying to impart a real thought or concern. It's progress, but not much.

3. Selective Listening

At this level we give our partner real attention—to a point. As long as the speaker is saying something we agree or sympathize with, we're with them. But if they switch direction and say something that doesn't jibe with us, we go back to pretend listening or ignoring them. It can be a reaction to a sentiment we have resistance toward, a story we don't care about, or a statement we disagree with. We initially sound like we're involved and concerned, but at a certain breakpoint we go back under our shell.

> *Person A:* I've had it up to here with the people at work. It's the refrigerator policy. I've said for weeks that if your name is on a container, it should be untouchable.

> *Person B:* I agree with you. People are still stealing your food?

> *Person A:* Yes. Someone is using my salad dressing.

> *Person B:* Oh, that's not good.

> *Person A:* I get what they're thinking. They think salad dressing is not really a piece of food. They think it's

more like a condiment. Like mustard and ketchup.

Person B: I guess I understand why people would think that way. You're only supposed to use a little bit of ketchup or mustard on something, whereas with salad dressing you probably use more at a time.

Person A: You know what? Even if there *is* a bottle of ketchup in the fridge, if *my* name is on that bottle, it's untouchable. If I feel like sharing my ketchup, I'll offer some.

Person B: But it's just ketchup.

Person A: So what? If my name is on it, the ketchup's off limits to anyone but me. If you need ketchup so badly, then hop over to the fast food joint and take a bunch of those ketchup packets. Leave mine alone.

Person B:

Person A: It's just the kind of disrespect that's so typical of how we live today! They think we should just throw ketchup around like it's something they're *entitled* to! I don't care! If I've declared that it's mine, you have to *ask* if you want to use it! You know?

Person B:

Person A: I said, "YOU KNOW?"

Person B: Oh, sorry. I was just looking at a squirrel on TV.

First, don't worry about how silly this exchange might sound. I made it silly on purpose. Person A is upset about something that many might consider a terribly trivial, very "first-world" problem. They're tired of a certain pattern and it's driving them crazy. Is it even worth the breath to complain about it?

The answer… doesn't matter. Whatever we think of Person A's obsession with ownership of foodstuffs, they're *upset* about what's happening. There is nothing wrong with feeling that way. It's Person A's feelings and they're entitled to feel any way they want about the refrigerator situation.

Person B agrees with Person A to a point. But then Person A says something that Person B doesn't agree with: that salad dressing and ketchup are, for all intents and purposes, not equals in the world of refrigerator leftovers. Person B thinks Person A's making a ridiculous point and has tuned them out.

Even if we *agree* with Person B and disagree with Person A, the fact is that when the conversation took a turn that Person B didn't like, they went back to level-1 ignorance of Person A. They just dropped out and stopped listening altogether.

That's selective listening: when the talk's going our way and resounding with our values, everything's great. But when we hear something that strikes us as wrong, we check out. It doesn't matter whether the topic is ketchup, world politics, family matters, or death—selective listening is still an incomplete level of communication (and some might consider it worse than ignorance).

4. Attentive Listening

This, in all honesty, is good. Not perfect but good. We're giving our partner our complete attention and listening to every detail they provide. We're not distracted, we're not shutting them out selectively, and we're not changing the subject.

However, what keeps this level from being five-star, fully focused listening is our analytical and judgmental mind. While they speak, we're comparing their statements to our own points of view, deciding whether we're in agreement with them or not, like someone on a debate team. This is more than fair in a two-way conversation where both parties are expected to provide equal exchange. But the fact that we're still assessing our partner with our own reason and logic keeps it from being pure listening:

> *Person A:* My mother is starting an online business.

> *Person B:* Doing what?

> *Person A:* Selling some of her homemade crafts. She thinks she can do it on her own. I'm not sure she's completely sure what she's in for.

Person B: What are your doubts?

Person A: That she's never done anything remotely related to web management or coding, and I don't know that she knows anyone who has. She's almost 70 and I'm just concerned she's underestimating what it will take.

Person B: You know, there are relatively cheap courses she can take online that can help her do it from scratch. It's helped a lot of people.

Person A: Yeah, I suppose she can look into those.

As you can see, this last exchange doesn't end in a disagreement, an invalidation, detachment, or, thankfully, another squirrel sighting. It's a fair and open exchange. Person B is paying close attention to what Person A is saying and is drawing Person A out so it's safe to reveal what their innermost feelings are. That's all good.

But after hearing Person A explain what their doubts are, Person B makes a suggestion that Person A's mom check out some online courses. Person B made this recommendation from their *own* standpoint. Hearing Person A's doubts activated Person B's own experience, judgment, or opinion, and it caused Person B to make a remark that was on topic but not reflective on what Person A was thinking or feeling.

Is this terrible? Of course not. Maybe Person A and Person B talk this way with each other all the time. They might be perfectly comfortable with giving and hearing each other's advice and might even welcome it. But Person A *could* have taken Person B's suggestion as a form of invalidation. Person A was in the midst of expressing her emotional state and may not have been finished—they could have taken Person B's advice as a forced solution intended to stop the conversation.

It all depends on how secure and close their relationship is and what boundaries they've set up for themselves in communication. Attentive listening is very good. Responses like Person B's aren't criminal and hopefully don't result in a spell of eggshell-walking when they're trying to figure out what to say. It's just something to be aware of, think about, and consider in advance of the communication.

5. Empathetic Listening

This is both the final, most desirable level of listening and the polar opposite of the first level of ignorance. In empathetic listening we give all our attention to the person we're talking to. We're not just zeroed in on what they're saying—we're putting ourselves in their shoes. We're not theorizing what *we* would do or feel in their situation; we're making a strong effort to understand where they're coming from.

In empathetic listening we react as though we're hearing our partner's story for the first time, even if it's something we've talked about before. We treat it as new and unusual information that doesn't pass through our own judgments, values, opinions, or frames of reference. It's not an easy level to achieve and requires discipline. But it's the most rewarding for both conversation partners.

Person A: I know we've talked about this before, but Chris is really getting to me. He's been a brat the last couple of weeks and I'm not sure what to do about it.

Person B: What is happening?

Person A: He's remote. He's emotionally distant. He's been staying out late most nights, and when he doesn't he locks himself into his study and shuts himself off.

Person B: You must feel extremely lonely.

Person A: Yeah, but more to the point, I just feel like I've been left out to dry. We've been together seven years and this sudden change just came out of nowhere. I'm confused. I don't know what brought it on. I don't know if he's hiding something from me or whether this is just what longtime couples go through.

Person B: You must be struggling to endure under that kind of mystery.

Person A: Yeah, I am. If I could get any clarity from him on the situation, it would be helpful. I don't know; we'll see.

In this example, Person B takes themselves out of the story completely. They start off by prompting Person A to confide in them. Then they're trying to imagine the emotional and mental state Person A is going through without making themselves the subject.

That's why they say, "*You must* feel extremely lonely" rather than "*I would feel* extremely lonely"—a small, maybe imperceptible difference in syntax, but one that reinforces that Person A is the subject of the exchange and that Person B is giving them their full focus.

Then Person B imagines being in Person A's position and tries to empathize: "You must be struggling to endure under that kind of mystery." This shows that Person B is really trying to understand what Person A is going through. That's different from the step in level 4, in which one compares what they're hearing with their own experience and judgments—it's a *guess*, not a declaration. And it's a "You" statement, not an "I" statement. That reminds Person A that they're getting full attention and comprehension, which in itself is a validating and positive communication experience.

Active Listening

Now that we know the five levels of listening and the stages from passive interest to total empathy, how do we get there? Just as learning to read and write takes practice, so does the art of active listening. Simply hearing someone isn't enough—you have to be very conscious and mindful of what skills you need to develop to be a great listener.

Active listening is one of the strongest relationship-building skills you can have. It establishes respect and concern for your partner's viewpoints and makes it easier for you to process information that's intricate and difficult to understand through passive listening. It also eases the communication process: active listening helps you get better informed on what the other person's needs are and therefore makes you less anxious and more open with your responses.

Listening involves more than your sense of hearing or sustaining eye contact. Your brain needs to compute several other aspects as well. In addition to understanding the speaker, you need to take other invisible factors into account: what their intentions might be, the context of the conversation, and even nonverbal signals and variations that you can't transcribe. At the same time, we have to push our ego out of the way so we can truly access what the other person is saying. We call this process "active" listening because it engages so many parts of our mind and makes us *do* something to understand what's being communicated.

Therapists (good ones, at least) are excellent models of how to be an active listener. They listen to their clients with a clear purpose. If there's something they're hearing that they're not 100% sure about, they encourage their clients to be clear and deliberate. They try to restate their patients' statements and ask them to elaborate on what they mean. Above all, they try to make their clients feel calm and safe about communicating through contemplation, clear body language, and a spirit of empathy.

Active listening involves a few essential elements that you can start concentrating on almost immediately.

Comprehending. The first step in active listening is, of course, understanding what the other person is saying in the first place. If the person who's talking to us is speaking the same language as we normally do, this process is fairly automatic. But there are other potential blocks—for example, if the person uses a lot of jargon or slang that we don't know or if there are differences in generation, social standing, or culture that we just don't know enough about.

A great thing to ask if we're not understanding what someone's saying is *"Can you explain it to me as if I were five years old?"* A five-year-old kid knows enough words to hold a conversation but needs to have relatively complex situations described to them in a very patient, deliberate way using the words that they already know. Especially if you think the other person fears appearing condescending or patronizing to you, asking them to describe something as if you were, let's say, *far younger than your actual age,* can make them feel a little more at ease.

Other statements asking for help comprehending include:

- "What happened?"

- "Tell me your story."

- "What do you mean?"

- "Tell me more."

Retaining. More than just remembering what you just heard, retaining information is understanding what the speaker is trying to say so we can give back a suitable reply.

Retaining isn't quite as simple as accurate recall. When we're listening to someone, we tend to retain only the details that strike us more personally or in ways that we're most used to retaining information. For example, if someone's telling us about a date they went on, we might be the kind that remembers the physical details of the event (what restaurant they went to, what movie they say, what they were wearing). Or we might recall some more general narrative about the date as a whole (what personality the other person had, what the date "felt like," how it compared to other dates in the past).

We're also inclined to retain "data" that would be more likely to elicit a response from us. In conversation we generally look for openings for us to say something to "get our two cents in." This is normal, but it's not entirely conducive to active listening. To properly retain what our conversation partner is telling us, we have to put our egos away and focus squarely on the other person's words. We can't act like we know the next thing they're going to say—we have to let them say it to complete their thoughts.

Retaining is also held back by a variety of things, including distractions, cognitive bias, or memory-related problems. To ensure you're getting all the relevant information you need, you could ask:

- "What does that mean to you?"

- "How did that make you feel?"

- "What was your reaction?"

Responding. Active listening requires an effort to form a knowing and proper response—otherwise, the speaker might feel like they're talking to a brick wall. An effective response will demonstrate our concern for what they're talking about. You're listening, comprehending, and retaining already; a quality response will prove that you *understand* everything they've said and picked up on their nonverbal communication.

Like retaining, it's important that a response isn't tinted with our own ego or ideas. You're trying to get a sense of the other person's feelings and opinions without biases you've developed:

> *Speaker A:* And that's why I don't like going to dinner parties.

Respondent B: That sounds insane! Were you flustered when that odd man jumped out of the cake?

Speaker A: Not flustered so much as disappointed. I expected something a little more grown-up from the Temperance League.

Respondent B: It must have tried your patience. Did it?

Speaker A: A little bit. But more than anything else, it just proved that I have to start putting some restrictions on the entertainment budget.

Responses in active listening should be reflective on what the speaker has said. They should display a deep interest in your partner's thoughts and feelings. Rather than shaping our *own* opinions and viewpoints, good responses in active listening help both parties make their own self-discoveries.

In issuing a quality response, try to reply to your partner's thoughts and feelings. You can do this by restating what they've said in your own words. Stay within their standpoint when you respond; introducing a suggestion or idea that doesn't have anything to do with their immediate situation could be too jarring or distracting. Don't offer a contradictory or conflicting opinion until you have fully understood, as much as you can, everything your partner is conveying to you. And even then, try to keep strong judgments tamped down.

Some positive responses in active listening might be:

- "I'm intrigued by your story."

- "That sounds like a ____ situation."

- "I can see how you'd feel that way."

- "I get the sense that you feel something has to change—what would you like to see happen?"

- "Do you feel anxious about this situation?"

The general goal of active listening is to fully grasp the viewpoint or life experience of the person who's speaking to you and for you to absorb that information in a meaningful way that could spur you to new knowledge and understanding. To accomplish the goals of comprehending, retaining, and responding, you can employ a few or more of these techniques:

Restating. Paraphrasing your partner's sentiments in your own words is an exceptional way to facilitate your comprehension. It's important *not* to simply repeat what they said back to you like a parrot, but rather to show that you've caught the essence of what they were saying.

> *Them:* That situation confused and scared me.

> *You:* It must have felt like a dangerous moment—it must have been hard to know what to do.

Reflecting. An alternative way of restating is to frame your reply along the lines of emotions rather than events or story points. Reflecting gives the speaker's story a deeper level that you can prove you have a handle on.

Them: So in the end, my dad said he knew all along I wouldn't get into that college.

You: That's terrible. That sounds like a cruel kind of rejection.

Summarizing. Try to verbally round up the details of a speaker's story into a concise form that displays that you get the whole picture.

You: So the baker got your order wrong, the dinner was burned, and they sent a hypnotist instead of a clown. Man, if that were *my* kid's birthday party, I'd feel ticked off!

Label emotions. Often, a speaker will just get lost in the practical and physical details of what they're relating to you. As sensitively as possible, try to identify the emotions they haven't been able to specifically verbalize yet.

Them: Finally my boss apologized for overlooking my work and assured me that he was going to pay more attention from now own.

> *You:* Wow, I'm guessing you feel pretty relieved and vindicated by that—not to mention a little cocky.

Probing. Without sounding like an invasive interrogator, try to ask leading questions that will elicit a deeper level of understanding and meaning from the person you're speaking with. Most people enjoy being asked questions that are well-formed and not too presumptuous.

> *You:* What did it feel like when that woman berated your kid at the supermarket? How did you *really* want to respond?

Silence. Frequently there's more to be said by a well-placed silence than by filling up the space with additional verbiage. Silence can give every participant a miniature bit of time to gather themselves and their thoughts. It could also help reduce the tension that could arise from a tense or fruitless interaction.

> *Them:* And *that's* when I decided skydiving wasn't my thing, especially when it's work-related.

You:

<u>*Not*</u> *sermonizing, giving unsolicited advice, or glibly reassuring.* Nobody likes to be put on a level secondary to someone else, and in communication, such a feeling might make the speaker feel like shutting down further discussion.

> *Them:* And worst of all, he cannot remember to put the toilet seat down.

> *Sermonizing you:* You should never have let him in your bathroom in the first place.

> *Unsolicited advising you:* You should barricade the bathroom until he agrees to your demands.

> *Glibly reassuring you:* Don't worry about it! Tomorrow's another lovely day full of wonderful possibilities.

Asking leading and open-ended questions. To show that you're invested in your partner's well-being, ask some nonbinary questions about their experience. These questions show that you're ready to get input and that you're interested in more than just the data or facts of a certain situation.

> *Them:* So I decided, after a couple hundred dollars later, perhaps parallel parking was something we were going to have to work a little harder on.

> *You:* How does that make you feel? What are your plans for learning? Where do you plan on doing it? What do you hope comes out of it?

Active listening takes a lot of patient work and practice and can even be challenging for people who are good at it. But it pays off in creating an atmosphere of true comprehension, easier information flow, and increased respect for all parties. It's communication at its highest.

Have Fewer Opinions

One aspect of shutting up and becoming a better listener is toning down your impulse to share your opinions. Have opinions, but understand that most of them are unnecessary anyway.

It's not just easier in this day and age to develop, share, and publicize our personal opinions—it can feel almost *mandatory* to have them. People in our time are generally feeling more strident and fervent about their convictions, to the point that they marginalize or even condemn people who have no views, or lukewarm ones at best, on a given topic.

Let me offer you a little bit of personal freedom if I can: you do *not* have to have opinions on everything. In fact, you don't even need to have opinions on issues that almost everyone else seems to have an opinion about. Refraining from having an opinion on every single subject not only frees the air of verbal clutter and static, but it also helps you become a better listener. It helps you key in on what other people are saying and helps you gain perspective you wouldn't otherwise be open to inside your belief bubble.

People have been arguing for centuries. Generations of opinions have come and gone, and the debates these opinions inspired haven't necessarily changed the outcome of our existence. What's more, regardless of your stance on a particular issue, it's still going to be there after you've finished expressing your opinion about it.

I'm not saying that you should shut up if there's an issue you feel particularly passionate about. I'm just saying that if you *don't* have an opinion on something, don't feel the pressure that you *need* to come up with one just to keep up with everyone else's.

If your friends all seem to have an opinion on something that you don't know much about, don't feel like you have to force yourself into having one. It's just as valuable to say something like "I don't know enough about that particular topic to offer an informed opinion."

I used to have to say that all the time. I had a number of friends who were deeply knowledgeable about advanced Internet technology. For some reason they assumed I did too. One of them just started talking to me about his opinions on the Linux operating system and what he saw as its strengths and limitations. He stopped several times to let me speak.

Finally I told him the truth: "I don't know anything about Linux. I have no opinion." My friend looked utterly shocked.

I was, at the time, considerably less computer literate than I am now. And to be honest I *still* don't use Linux, though I know a little bit more about it—but still not enough to have an informed opinion about it.

Opinions about operating systems are considerably less volatile and antagonistic than views on the more divisive issues of today. But even when you're feeling the pressure to "draw a line in the sand" about a topic that you don't feel up to speed on, it's fairer for everyone to acknowledge you don't know enough to say so definitively. (For the record, that guy and I remain friends today.)

And even if you *do* have well-informed, passionate opinions about something, to be a better listener you may have to consider your audience. Like I said, the objects you have opinions about will still be around after you're done talking about them. And feeling too strongly about certain less vital things—musical preferences, scientific analyses, whether your favorite baseball team is being mismanaged, etc.—won't really change those any of those realities (unless you're a music executive, research scientist, or baseball manager—and even *they're* not guaranteed to have an impact).

Sometimes exchanging these less consequential opinions with others is fun. That's why we have sports talk radio and podcasts about everything. But it's sometimes tempting to conjure an opinion simply because we notice a bunch of other people being passionate about it and we feel left out. I personally think people are more likely to respect someone who doesn't have opinions on trivial matters and admits as much rather than someone who makes up an opinion just to keep in the conversation.

That's why it's a totally reasonable option to let yourself go of opinions that ultimately don't mean anything—which, as you can see, is almost all of them. You don't have to let someone else's musical tastes, aesthetic choices, or parenting styles ruin your time on earth. You don't have to let someone else's passionate and different point of view become an outrageous insult on your character—especially if you don't know those people personally.

Letting those useless opinions go will give you less to defend yourself about. They'll take less of your energy and won't sap up your resources for more important things like connecting with other people and being a good listener. And they'll give more room to you to develop the opinions that actually *do* matter—the ones that are true life-or-death, pressing, and true concerns.

Takeaways:

- The art of shutting up and allowing other people to communicate is otherwise known as listening. Are you listening in your interactions, or are you simply waiting for your turn to speak? This is an important distinction, as the former creates flowing conversation and the latter creates battling monologues.

There are many aspects of listening that are similar to validation, as they are focused on providing a specific positive outcome.

- The five stages of listening are ignoring, pretend listening, selective listening, attentive listening, and empathetic listening. Most of us are stuck in the first three levels. Some of us might reach level 4 from time to time.

- Active listening is another aspect that gives people the distinct sense that they are being heard and seen. It ideally consists of comprehending, retaining, responding, and restating. The goal is to go deeper and have people talk as much as possible. Silence is also a useful tool for this goal.

- Finally, when seeking to listen better, attempt to shed some of your opinions that make you want to interrupt people or talk over them. The truth is, most opinions are unnecessary or useless. They make you come in with a specific angle or preconception, neither of which are helpful in communication and relationships.

Chapter 6. Dig Deep

Think back to the last time you met someone new at a networking event or party. What was the first thing out of your mouth? You might not remember it, but you can probably predict it. It was likely one of the following:

- Where are you from?
- Who do you know here?
- How was your weekend?
- Where did you go to school?
- What do you do?

These are normal questions to begin communication—so normal in fact that you probably did predict all of them. We ask them instinctively because they are supposedly good at breaking the ice.

We are searching for the "*me too!*" moment that can spark a deeper discussion. We're searching for commonalities and shared experiences.

If we ask the question, "Where did you go to school?" we are hoping they attended the same university as us, or a university where we have mutual friends. The next natural question we always ask is a variation of "Oh wow! What a small world. Do you know James Taylor? He also went there around your time."

While you may not realize that you are always hunting for similarities, they, more than almost anything, set the stage for successful communication. As much as we would like to think that we are open-minded and can get along with people from every background and origin, the reality is that we usually get along best with people who we think are like us. In fact, we seek them out.

It's why Little Italy, Chinatown, and Koreatown exist. It's why we get irrationally excited at the prospect of having a mutual friend with a stranger. But I'm not just talking about race, skin color, religion, or sexual orientation. I'm talking about people who share our values, look at the world the same way we do, and have the same perspective on life. As the old saying goes, birds of a feather flock together.

Similarities make us relate better to other people because we think they'll understand us on a deeper level than other people. If we share at least one significant similarity, then all sorts of positive traits follow, because we typically have a positive self-image, and we see them as our contemporary, essentially an extension of ourselves. When you think someone is on your level, you want to connect with them because they will probably understand you better than most.

Suppose you were born in a small village in South Africa. The population of the village ranges from 900 to 1,000 people. You now live in London and you are attending a party at a friend's home. You meet someone that also happens to be from that small village in South Africa. This person is just eight years older, so you never encountered each other.

What warm feelings will you immediately have toward this other person, and what assumptions will you make about them? How interested will you be in connecting with them and spending more time together in the future? What inside jokes or specialized points of reference can you discuss that you haven't ever been able to with anyone else?

Hopefully that illustration drives home the value of similarity and how it drives connection. We typically use the small talk questions mentioned at the top of this chapter to find similarity, but there are better, more effective ways to find similarities with people.

When we go deep and get more detail about people, we find more and more to like, and our communications always benefit. Likewise, when we stay on the surface, everyone appears to be boring and vanilla, including us. It's just hard to get excited by another face in the crowd, and that's what staying on small talk topics makes out of everyone.

So to improve your communication, it's imperative to go deeper than you thought possible or necessary with people. It can be uncomfortable and you might feel like you're prying, but going deep doesn't mean that you assume the position of head interrogator. If anything, direct and invasive questions can cause people to clam up quickly.

But when you are the first to go deep, divulge, and share about yourself, it sends a powerful message to others. The first part of this chapter will focus on how you can start to dig deep into yourself and how that can translate into your interactions. It doesn't necessarily mean you are talking about yourself nonstop like you would during a cathartic therapy session—just that you share more than you normally would. After all, you can only control what you do, not necessarily how others will respond.

You went skiing last month.

You went skiing last month with your two brothers and you almost broke your foot.

Which of those stories is easier to relate to, find a similarity with, and overall know someone better with? Obviously, it's the second version since there is literally three times as much information. It didn't take much more effort, and it took literally only four seconds of your time.

If you are having trouble connecting with others, it's likely you are expecting to find a similarity without sharing anything about yourself. It's a cycle, because if you don't share, other people won't feel compelled to share, and thus there is exponentially less chance of finding a similarity to connect over. You have to become comfortable being the first to share information, even if it seems scary or like you are opening yourself up for judgment and rejection. But when you take on the burden, you make people feel safe enough to share about themselvcs.

An easy way to break into this habit is to never give one-word answers and always provide context for a remark by using three distinct details.

The example from above works well to illustrate this.

You went skiing. This is as good as a one-word answer and it doesn't provide much, if any, context. If you went skiing, you can surely provide the occasion and circumstances surrounding it.

You went skiing last month with your two brothers and you almost broke your foot. This is an exponentially better answer because you provided two details: you talked about your family and you talked about one of the notable events of the ski trip.

If sharing even this amount of detail feels uncomfortable and unnatural for you, it's a sign you are probably the cause for your unmemorable communication. You are essentially dropping the conversational ball when it is hit back to you. You may be the cause of awkward silence more often than not, because others will expect a back and forth flow, but they end up doing all the work while you wonder what's wrong.

In other words, get used to this feeling of discomfort because it's something you need to improve upon. Your comfort zone is currently too small to be conducive to open dialogue. The feeling that you are oversharing needs to stop because it keeps your guard up unintentionally, and not many people will make the effort to fight through the guard.

Now you may wonder what to share. What kind of information should you disclose to others? Is it as simple as giving out three details instead of one? No, that's just a starting point. But where is the line? What information is TMI (too much information) and will disgust or repulse others? What information is beneficial to share with others and enhances lines of communication? What should you keep private?

Here's a better question—what do you talk about with your friends? You probably overshare without shame or inhibition. They may laugh, gag, or declare "I didn't need to know that!" But they still share everything, because that's the dynamic of a friendship. So even if you feel that you are entering TMI territory, that is still better than not disclosing anything because you are still treating others like your friends. Outside of a strict professional environment, the boundaries between you and sharing exist only in your mind.

Share what is on your mind. This might include personal details or controversial opinions. Share slowly at first to gauge people's responses, but once you get the sense that someone is on the same page and willing to befriend you as well, you can open the floodgates, so to speak.

The more you reveal about yourself, the more connection points you generate with the other person. You reveal things you like or dislike, which the other person may be able to relate to and disagree or agree with.

You can find more things in common as you reveal your preferences, opinions, loves, hates, likes, dislikes, sensitivities, memories, emotions, thoughts, and anecdotes.

Share your emotions. The reason emotions are so powerful is because they are universal. Scientific studies have shown that people from different cultures can recognize what smiles and frowns mean, which indicates that all people feel and express emotions in similar ways. You become more human and relatable when you express your emotions, and you've just made it acceptable to venture into an area that can be scary for others. They'll reciprocate because you took the first daring step.

This can start with talking about how happy or sad something makes you—that's all it takes to open a deeper dialogue.

Share stories from your own life. Again, this makes you seem more relatable. Even though it doesn't feel like it, we all go through similar circumstances and struggles every day. We all brush our teeth, hate waking up, and commute to some kind of job. You have some part of your life story that others can relate to. This makes people feel closer to you and lets them laugh and talk about how they went through the same thing. Often, they will start to tell their stories based on yours.

We all have common experiences. We all remember when we learned to ride a bike, embarrassing moments in high school, or disasters in dating.

If you know certain topics are going to come up (and we can *always* predict small talk questions), you can make matters easier on yourself by brainstorming stories beforehand. You can rehearse them, which means you don't have to do all of this in the spur of the moment.

"How was your weekend?"

Prepare a better answer beforehand: *"I saw a movie about a dog who dies. I'll admit I cried, but so did everyone else in the theater. I went to a pet shop after and bought my guinea pig a new toy just to show him how much I appreciate him."*

If you break it down, most great conversations are exchanges of interrelated stories that build upon each other. Rehearsing your stories comes with the added benefit of allowing you to be whoever you want to be. If you wish to present yourself a certain way, you can simply filter your stories to reflect those characteristics. For example, if you wish to showcase your outdoorsy spirit, you can make sure your stories revolve around camping and hiking trips.

"How was your weekend?"

"I didn't do much but I started to plan my next camping trip. I'm thinking it will be about two weeks in the mountains nearby. It'll be a longer trip than usual but it's exciting because I'll be catching all of my food."

If you don't feel like you have an answer to a question, get creative. You don't have to answer the literal question in front of you.

As long as you address the question asked in some way, that's good enough because people don't care about the literal answer anyway. They care that an interesting dialogue is happening, and that they are a part of it.

Share your flaws and vulnerabilities. People are typically fond of the fact that I was overweight as a kid. At times, my arms resembled tires from all the folds I had, and the hilarious proof is my third-grade photo where my face appeared to be almost twice the width of the face of the child sitting next to me. When I stumbled upon it again recently, I thought there might have been a photo processing issue that smeared my face, but alas, it was true to life.

I was a fat kid and I'm not ashamed to admit it. I'm completely transparent about it, and I'm okay with being honest about my issues with my weight. Why are people fond of this fact I would seemingly want to conceal as much as possible?

Because it shows vulnerability. Vulnerability is uncertainty. You are dangling yourself for judgment and rejection. Naturally, we tend to avoid vulnerability because it can be frightening, but it will typically be better for you than not.

Vulnerability has an amazing effect on other people: it makes them want to open up as well. When you show vulnerability first, you create an open space that appears to be free of judgment. How often is it that you've admitted something embarrassing, only for the person you are speaking with to admit the same thing or worse?

Many people seek a space to be vulnerable and speak without any pretenses or filters, and you can give them that space by showing your imperfections. Again, we run into the theme that you are just seeking to communicate instead of impressing or appearing a certain way.

Ultimately, you want to just get into the habit of talking about yourself more and sharing things you wouldn't necessarily think about sharing. Digging deep starts with you.

It can be intimidating. You have been taught your whole life to be modest, not talk about yourself, and even remain private. It feels like you are going against years of teachings. You may worry that you are bothering others or overstepping boundaries. But remember, there is a significant difference between focusing on yourself and divulging personal information to give people something to relate to.

Ask Better Questions

Especially (but not exclusively) with people we're just getting to know, questions are excellent ways to give our communications depth and reinforce our connections. Unfortunately, most questions we use just don't get anywhere. Some of them are made lazily, which prompts lazy answers in return. Most of them aren't geared at digging deep and understanding people.

Good questions help both parties develop deeper communication. Well-constructed inquiries can help a respondent find new ways to think about their situations, which strengthens trust and keeps communication fresh. Thankfully, asking good questions is a practice that's completely within your power.

Researcher Arthur Aron conducted a study in 1997, in which he paired students who didn't know each other and gave them a list of fairly personal questions to ask. Although the questions were not offensively intrusive, they were more than just small talk ("Would you like to be famous and how?" "Do you have a secret hunch about how you will die?" "What is your most terrible memory?" "How do you feel about your relationship with your mother?").

Aron found that the students responded to these "deep dives" with more openness and intimacy. The students didn't feel that the questions, as personal as they were, necessarily invaded their privacy or weakened them in any way. Instead, they encouraged honesty, more emotional fluency, and sincerity in the respondents. They felt closer to the other participants, who were complete strangers before the experiment. The implications were clear:

going more deeply or intensely in our communications can create positive results far more swiftly than one might think.

Coming up with effective questions isn't necessarily a reflexive act that we can do on the fly. To get more revealing answers that build depth and improve intimate relationships, here are six strategies that can be of great help in digging deep and learning about people.

1. Ask open-ended questions. Questions that require only yes or no answers will usually produce nothing more than yes or no answers. If the question contains no prompt for the responder to elaborate, there's a very good chance they won't.

Open-ended questions, though, can spark discussions and bring up new, revelatory understandings that binary questions don't encourage. For example, instead of asking *"Are you satisfied* with your relationship with your mother?" you could ask *"Why is* your relationship with your mother the way it is? *How* did it get that way?"

2. Get behind assumptions. We all operate through our own personal experiences, knowledge, and assumptions—you know what you know. Good communication involves understanding *someone else's* beliefs. When they speak about issues that are unfamiliar to us, we ask them to explain what they mean, what they believe, or what assumptions they bring to the situation.

Well-worded questions can bridge that gap: "How did you come to that conclusion?" "What makes this particular situation different from normal?" "What gave you this idea?" "What's the story behind your belief?" When you sense a gap between what your partner is saying and what you're familiar with, that's the time to get clarity on what they're basing their statements on.

3. Get all sides of the story. There are very few situations in life that are uncomplicated or cut-and-dried. No matter how strongly someone feels about their particular viewpoint, there's always more than one side to a given story. By getting as much information as we possibly can about a certain topic or story, we get deeper and more understanding about the total nature of a situation, problem, or event.

This is often a case of not shutting out opinions or beliefs that might threaten or offend us, which in this day can be very difficult to do. But a responsibly asked question will help get a better picture of the greater context of things and will help us understand matters beyond our own limited view. "Is there another perspective on this situation?" "What are some of the things someone who disagrees with you would say?" "What would happen if someone did this differently?"

In general, don't be satisfied that you've gotten absolutely every fact of a certain matter to make an informed assumption.

4. Ask follow-up questions. When we're trying to get close to someone, a lot of the questions we may ask of them don't have easy answers. In fact, if we were writing them out, they'd probably be more like two- or three-part questions with room to elaborate.

In personal interactions, we can emulate that depth—and show the strength of our focus—by asking follow-up questions. But they don't have to come immediately after your partner's answered. One author (me) suggests seeing how many questions you can ask in a row without offering any comment of your own so you can allow your partner to expand their response more and keep digging deeper.

It's very important *not* to sound too much like a journalist or an inquisitor when asking follow-up questions. Instead, try to link your respondent's answers to things they've already discussed: "What you just said about not fully understanding computer technology reminds me of what you said about not doing well in school. How do those relate?" or "How did that breakup affect your views on relationships?"

Good follow-up questions will make you sound invested in your partner's response—and it may take a while for you to get to the answers you both need to know. But that's more time spent communicating.

5. Get comfortable with "dead air." People tend to be scared to death of "awkward silences"—those moments in conversation when there's a pregnant pause and nobody says anything. We tend to misinterpret these silences as a sign that either we or our partner has run out of things to say. Sometimes that's true. But sometimes, it's someone trying to gauge you and subtly seek permission to keep talking.

Thus, silence can work in communication's favor—when you're at ease with silence and don't rush to fill it yourself with inane chatter, you'll be prompting people to speak more and more. Think of it as seeing if moments of silence can help them generate their own, new thoughts and help the conversation get to a deeper level. This is perhaps the easiest part of digging deeper; give people the space to do it for themselves instead of at your asking.

6. Encourage your partner to come up with their own insights. The best kinds of question-and-answer sessions aren't just one way, with one person providing insight and information to the other one. It's always best—and far more conducive to good communication—when *everyone's* learning new things.

Questions that encourage self-discovery are, without exception, far more productive than questions that originate from a specific point of view. "What did you learn from that experience navigating the Amazon River? What do you think it gave you for your life?" Or perhaps "What would you want to say to your father if he were still alive?"

Like all questions, those intended to promote self-discovery need to be carefully considered. You never want to sound like you're on an inquisition, and it's easy to fall into that trap without trying. Especially with interpersonal relationships, you need to strike that balance of getting information while being supportive. If that strikes you as being too accommodating to someone's feelings—well, maybe personal relationships just aren't for you.

Externalities

So you're starting or deepening a personal relationship. You're being upfront with each other about yourselves. You're asking questions that are specifically related to your personal histories and innermost feelings.

Fortunately, going deep doesn't necessarily have to be so direct as asking "What is your deepest fantasy and wildest dream?" Even the techniques we just discussed about asking questions aren't always applicable or helpful.

As important as that step is, it can also be exhausting. It can also be *exhaustive*—theoretically, once you've talked about events and subjects only pertinent to your own lives, you'll run out of things to discover about yourself and the other person. There are only so many high school proms, parental arguments, complicated work scenarios, and family reunions you'll get in one life. In the worst-case scenario, it will turn into a job interview gone awry.

We are, of course, generally disposed to talk about ourselves and the things we've directly experienced or shared. But there's a considerable amount of insight to be obtained by talking about subjects and events external to your life. Author Daniel Menaker straightforwardly calls this approach turning the conversation toward "third things—not me, not them, but something else." It's not about you or the other person in particular. It's just about something external, even as benign as the news of the day or the types of ferns that you are surrounded by. Call it enlightened small talk.

Talking about external things serves as an inroad to discovering how somebody really feels and believes.

If you directly ask someone personal details about themselves, their answers are often flat or inadequate. Imagine someone (other than a therapist) asking, "Tell me about when you feel angry" or "What do you believe in?" In addition to just sounding like left-field questions, they're not likely to elicit very lucid responses. Some might find the questions a bit intrusive or nosy, especially in the early stages of a relationship.

When you bring up things that are happening in the world, you actually *get* answers to those questions through others' reactions to those external situations. Their opinions and feedback offer clues to the way they really are without feeling on-the-spot or awkward. Discussing external things can help you get a more complete picture of what makes up the person you're with, and they're exceptionally helpful because there's no limit to what you can talk about. For an example of the type of deeper information you can glean indirectly, consider asking someone, "Where do you get your news? What kind of publications you read most of the time?"

It's an innocent question, and it's something external. Yet you can learn much about someone's views, preferences, values, and overall worldview by knowing their reference sources and preferred viewpoints. This is useful far beyond any political purpose—you immediately understand how someone likes to see the world when you know what media they tend to consume.

Instead of digging deep directly, which is often off-putting or awkward at best, you can dig deep by measuring people's reactions to external things. You'll often get a more honest answer, and you'll learn more about them in the process.

Takeaways:

- The value of digging deep can't be overstated. Digging deep is really the act of forging friendships and building deeper relationships. This is how you move past being an acquaintance and gain access to people's inner circles.

- The first means to digging deep is to reveal more details about yourself. Someone has to act first, and it might as well be you. The reality is that you are probably not sharing much while expecting others to pour their hearts out for you. So make a rule of sharing three details in every applicable response. This gives you a greater chance of finding similarities, which are easy to bond over—in particular, share emotions, vulnerabilities, and stories from your life.

- At the same time as sharing more about yourself, it's imperative to learn how to ask better questions of people. This way, you're digging deep with yourself and with others—showing your true self and knowing how to get them to reciprocate. A few insights include asking open-ended questions, getting behind assumptions, getting the full story or multiple perspectives, always following up, getting comfortable with silence, and trying to help people find their own insights.

- Finally, even though great questions create great responses, it can be exhausting and exhaustive. Sometimes we must turn to externalities—topics that are neither about you nor the other person. This is helpful in two main ways. This allows you to indirectly probe and learn about others; asking directly sometimes causes people to clam up or otherwise provide guarded answers. When you measure people's responses to external topics, you can gain greater insight into them just by understanding the values and perspectives involved in those responses.

Speaking and Coaching

Imagine going far beyond the contents of this book and dramatically improving the way you interact with the world and the relationships you'll build.

Are you interested in contacting Patrick for:

- A social skills workshop for your workplace
- Speaking engagements on the power of conversation and charisma
- Personalized social skills and conversation coaching

Patrick speaks around the world to help people improve their lives through the power of building relationships with improved social skills. He is a recognized industry expert, bestselling author, and speaker.

To invite Patrick to speak at your next event or to inquire about coaching, get in touch directly through his website's contact form at http://www.PatrickKingConsulting.com/contact, or contact him directly at Patrick@patrickkingconsulting.com.

Cheat Sheet

Chapter 1. It's All About Your Approach

- Communication is tough. But it all starts with the way you think about it. It's your approach—your mindset. Only then can the tips and tactics you'll learn later be of any use. What kind of patterns of thought will benefit you in your quest for better communication and closer ties?

- First, be intentional about your communication and engagement. Relationships aren't built on luck; they're built on you taking the initiative. Every relationship needs to escape a certain threshold of interest, and often, you must find yourself making the first move.

- Second, change the goal you have when communicating with people. Too many of us are fixated on impressing people. This backfires in many ways. Instead, change your goal to engage or entertain others, which are pursuits that keep other people as the top priority.

- Third, stay curious about people. Admittedly, this is hard because we just don't feel others are always worth our time. But this, in and of itself, is a mindset to snap out of. Ask yourself what people can teach you, what is unique about people, and what similarities you have. If all else fails, make a game out of discovering people.

Chapter 2. Reading Between the Lines

- Communication really is not about the words coming out of our mouths. For better or worse, we really communicate through indirect means. Perhaps this was an evolutionary reaction to avoiding confrontation or developing social skills; whatever the case, we need to learn to read between the lines to communicate effectively.

- A large piece of that puzzle is to understand subtext. What is subtext? It's taking into account everything *except* the explicit words that are spoken—the words are overt, whereas subtext is an overt communication. It's looking at context, personal history, tone of voice, body language, and delivery to interpret a message that could very well be the complete opposite from the explicit words you hear. Just imagine how you tend to understand the motivations and intentions of movie and book characters without them directly saying or thinking it.

- Specific pieces of subtext that are relatively universal are social cues. For our purposes, some of the most useful cues are about people's interest or lack thereof. Look at people's general responsiveness, chattiness, silence, and body positioning.

- Empathy is the final piece of reading between the lines. In a sense, it prevents you from having to do so, because when you think in terms of empathy, you innately understand people's emotions and thoughts. This allows you to know what people are thinking without having to necessarily analyze subtext or take context into account. You can achieve this by focusing on a five-step thought process that humanizes the other person and makes them more relatable.

Chapter 3. Good Vibrations

- Sometimes the best method of communication isn't about the words themselves; it's about the feelings you create in others. To that end, positivity and good vibrations are important to open and clear lines for rapport.

- Compliments are the first way to create positivity and goodwill. They take less effort than you might expect, and it sometimes just requires thinking out loud. There are two levels of compliments: superficial observations and ones that create a deeper impact based on people's conscious choices.

- Another way to create positivity is to become a giver. Giving is about getting into the habit of anticipating the needs and desires of other people. However, just stick to five-minute favors. Overall, ask yourself if you can leave the other person in a better condition than you found them. Once you make that your intention, you will begin to approach people differently.

- The final layer of giving is to understand the five love languages, which are particular methods of giving and showing your attention and care. The languages are words of affirmation, physical touch, giving gifts, quality time, and acts of service.

- The final aspect of creating positivity is to manage your negative emotions. This is difficult—one of the most difficult tasks for a human. But the act of biting your tongue more can make people feel safer and more comfortable around you, rather than avoiding you like a ticking time bomb. You must also seek to quell your judgmental tendencies, because otherwise people will associate you with negative feelings.

Chapter 4. Validation and Respect

- Validation is the act of showing respect and acknowledgment to people's intentions and emotions. It can be as easy as nodding your head, but it can also go much deeper for greater impact and respect.

- At the most basic level, it consists of identifying people's emotions and then justifying them. You first act as a detective to understand what you are dealing with and then make people feel that they are completely rational in feeling their emotions. Emotions are never quite rational, but they are always real.

- Many times when we try to validate, we are actually worsening the situation by using invalidating statements. These are statements that dismiss or minimize people's feelings, such as "Oh, you'll be fine" or "You shouldn't feel that way!" They feel more prescriptive and try to convince people to see the bright side of things—but that's not what they are interested in at the moment.

- A helpful six-step path to validation is as follows: being present, accurately reflecting emotions, guessing emotions, understanding emotions in context, affirming emotions, and then being honest.

- Validation is one of the ultimate shows of respect. But there are other ways to subtly show respect and caring for others. They center around awareness, action, appreciation, and, most importantly, attention.

Chapter 5. Shut Up and Listen

- The art of shutting up and allowing other people to communicate is otherwise known as listening. Are you listening in your interactions, or are you simply waiting for your turn to speak? This is an important distinction, as the former creates flowing conversation and the latter creates battling monologues. There are many aspects of listening that are similar to validation, as they are focused on providing a specific positive outcome.

- The five stages of listening are ignoring, pretend listening, selective listening, attentive listening, and empathetic listening. Most of us are stuck in the first three levels. Some of us might reach level 4 from time to time.

- Active listening is another aspect that gives people the distinct sense that they are being heard and seen. It ideally consists of comprehending, retaining, responding, and restating. The goal is to go deeper and have people talk as much as possible. Silence is also a useful tool for this goal.

- Finally, when seeking to listen better, attempt to shed some of your opinions that make you want to interrupt people or talk over them. The truth is, most opinions are unnecessary or useless. They make you come in with a specific angle or preconception, neither of which are helpful in communication and relationships.

<u>Chapter 6. Dig Deep</u>

- The value of digging deep can't be overstated. Digging deep is really the act of forging friendships and building deeper relationships. This is how you move past being an acquaintance and gain access to people's inner circles.

- The first means to digging deep is to reveal more details about yourself. Someone has to act first, and it might as well be you. The reality is that you are probably not sharing much while expecting others to pour their hearts out for you. So make a rule of sharing three details in every applicable response. This gives you a greater chance of finding similarities, which are easy to bond over—in particular, share emotions, vulnerabilities, and stories from your life.

- At the same time as sharing more about yourself, it's imperative to learn how to ask better questions of people. This way, you're digging deep with yourself and with others—showing your true self and knowing how to get them to reciprocate. A few insights include asking open-ended questions, getting behind assumptions, getting the full story or multiple perspectives, always following up, getting comfortable with silence, and trying to help people find their own insights.

- Finally, even though great questions create great responses, it can be exhausting and exhaustive. Sometimes we must turn to externalities—topics that are neither about you nor the other person. This is helpful in two main ways. This allows you to indirectly probe and learn about others; asking directly sometimes causes people to clam up or otherwise provide guarded answers. When you measure people's responses to external topics, you can gain greater insight into them just by understanding the values and perspectives involved in those responses.

www.ingramcontent.com/pod-product-compliance
Lightning Source LLC
Chambersburg PA
CBHW070922030426
42336CB00014BA/2491